BALLADS

of the

NORTH AND *SOUTH*

IN THE

CIVIL WAR

BALLADS

of the

NORTH AND SOUTH

IN THE

CIVIL WAR

Walbrook D. Swank
Colonel, USAF, RET.

 Burd Street Press

Walbrook D. Swank, USAF Ret.
Rt. 2, Box 433
Mineral, VA. 23117

This Burd Street Press book
was printed by
Beidel Printing House, Inc.
63 West Burd Street
Shippensburg, PA 17257 USA

In respect for the scholarship contained herein, the acid-free paper used in this book meets the guidelines for permanence and durability of the Committee on Production Guidelines for Book Longevity of the Council on Library Resources.

For a complete list of available publications
please write
White Mane Publishing Company, Inc.
P.O. Box 152
Shippensburg, PA 17257 USA

Library of Congress Cataloging-in-Publication Data

Ballads of the North and South in the Civil War / [compiled by]
      Walbrook D. Swank.
            p.   cm.
            ISBN 1-57249-002-0 (alk. paper)
            1.   United States--History--Civil War, 1861-1865--Poetry.
      2.   United States--History--Civil War, 1861-1865--Songs and
      music--Texts.   3.   Confederate States of America--Songs and
      music--Texts.   4.   Confederate States of America--History--
      Poetry.   5.   Ballads, English--United States--Texts.   6. Songs,
      English--United States--Texts.   7.   War-songs--United States--
      Texts.   8. American poetry--19th century.   9. War poetry,
      American.   I.   Swank, Walbrook D.   (Walbrook Davis)
      PS595.C55B35   1996
      811'.04408358--dc20
                                                            95-51408
                                                                  CIP

Also by the Author

Clash of Sabres—Blue and Gray

The War and Louisa County, 1861–1865

Train Running for the Confederacy, 1861–1865
An Eyewitness Memoir

Confederate War Stories, 1861–1865

Eyewitness to War, 1861–1865

Courier for Lee and Jackson

Battle of Trevilian Station

My WW II Diary and The War Effort

CIVIL WAR STORIES
Anecdotes-Letters-Memoirs

and the
Award Winning

Confederate Letters and Diaries
1861–1865

Dedication

To Civil War Re-enactors, North and South, who Keep the
Memories Of this Epoch Alive.

Contents

CHAPTER I
BALLADS OF THE NORTH

CHAPTER II
BALLADS OF THE SOUTH

About the Author

During his distinguished career in the United States Air Force the author received numerous awards for meritorious service and at one time was a member of a Task Force in the Office of the Personnel Advisor to the President, The White House.

His grandfather, Thomas S. Davis of Richmond, Virginia, was member of the Tenth Virginia Cavalry and a relative of President Jefferson Davis. He has written or edited ten previous books, all but one, about the North-South conflict, including his Award Winning Confederate Letters and Diaries, 1861-1865.

He has a master's degree in American Military History and holds membership in Bonnie Blue Society which is based on his scholarly research and published literature. He is the recipient of the United Daughters of the Confederacy's Jefferson Davis medal for his outstanding contributions to the preservation and promotion of our Southern history and heritage.

He is a member of the Society of Civil War Historians , the Military Order of the Stars and Bars, Sons of the American Revolution, the Ohio State Alumni Association and four Virginia historical societies.

Acknowledgement

The material in this book is derived from the work of an anonymous Union veteran of the American Civil War.

Introduction

Ballads tell a story in the form of a poem. Minstrels during the Middle Ages told of some heroic deed, romance or event or legend that many times originated among the common people. Originally, ballads were meant to be sung and were developed by people who shared the same beliefs, habits and ideas for generations.

This tradition of handing down beliefs, legends and stories in this manner was accelerated in many countries during tragic and momentous periods of upheaval and turmoil. This was especially true during the era of the American Civil War.

This outstanding collection of ballads of the North and South includes war stories, war songs, sectional patriotism, individual sentimentalism and patriotic themes that reflect the thoughts and feelings of a nation of people split asunder by the ravages of war.

BALLADS

of

THE NORTH

Ballads of the War

GOD SAVE THE NATION!
By Theodore Tilton

THOU who ordainest, for the land's salvation,
Famine, and fire, and sword, and lamentation,
Now unto Thee we lift our supplication—
    God save the Nation!

By the great sign, foretold, of Thy Appearing,
Coming in clouds, while mortal men stand fearing,
Show us, amid this smoke of battle, clearing,
    Thy chariot nearing!

By the brave blood that floweth like a river,
Hurl Thou a thunderbolt from out Thy quiver!
Break Thou the strong gates! Every letter shiver!
    Smite and deliver!

Slay Thou our foes, or turn them to derison!—
Then, in the blood-red Valley of Decision,
Make the land green with Peace, as in a vision
    Of fields Elysian!

A path to the country where Freedom abides!
Division! No, never? The Union forever!
And cursed be the hand that our country would
    sever?

The Union! The Union! In God we repose!
    We confide in the power that vanquished our foes!
The God of our fathers. Oh, still may He be
    The strength of the Union, the hope of the free!
Division! No, never! The Union forever!
    And cursed be the hand that our country would
        sever!

FLAG OF THE CONSTELLATION
By T. Buchanan Read

THE stars of morn on our banner borne
    With the iris of heaven are blended;
The hand of our sires first mingled those fires
    And by us they shall be defended.

CHORUS
Then hail the true Red, White, and Blue,
    The flag of the constellation;
It sails as it sailed by our forefathers hailed,
    O'er battles that made us a nation.

What hand so bold, as strike from its fold,
    One star or one stripe of its bright'ning?
For him be those stars each a fiery Mars,
    Each stripe be a terrible lightning.
        Then hail the true Red.

Its meteor form shall ride the storm,
    Till the fiercest of foes surrender;
The storm gone by, it shall gild the sky,
    A rainbow of peace and of splendor
        Then hail the true Red.

Peace to the world, is our motto unfurled,
   Though we shun not the field that is gory;
At home or abroad, fearing none but our god,
   We will carve our own pathway to glory.
   Then hail the true Red.

WAR SONG
By William H. C. Hosmer

WITH sword on thigh, "to do or die,"
   I march to meet the foe;
A pirate band have cursed the land,
   Then deal the deadly blow.
To Richmond on, and write upon
   Her walls the words of doom;
Secession's horde from Freedom's sword,
   Deserves a bloody tomb.

Sound, bugle, sound; a rally round
   The Star-flag of the Free;
Nursed by a flood of generous blood
   Was Freedom's sacred tree.
Accursed by God in dust he trod
   Rebellion's hellish horde;
The fiends to tame hearts are aflame
   With cannon peal and sword.

'Tis hard to leave the babes that grieve
   For a fond, absent sire;
His cherished wife, charm of his life
   To brave the battle's fire.
But duty calls, and loudly falls
   Our war-cry on the ear;
Our banners wave above the brave—
   Then on! and know not fear.

HE SLEEPS WHERE HE FELL
ANONYMOUS

HE sleeps where he fell 'mid the battle's roar,
   With his comrades true and brave;
And his noble form we shall see no more,—
   It rests in a hero's grave:
Where the rebel foe in his might came forth,
   With all his power and pride;
And our gallant men from the rugged North
   Like patriots fought and died.

He sleeps near the hill where bright flowers grow,
   In the wildest woodland shade;
Where the valley stream, in the dell below,
   With an echo fills the glade;
Where the boasting lines of the traitor-South
   Filed up, o'er the grassy banks,
Till the bursting shells from our cannon's mouth
   Flung death in their broken ranks.

He sleeps 'neath the sod where I prayerfully knelt,
   While the enemy round me stood,
As I took from the corse his battle-belt,
   Still wet with his heart's warm blood;
And the summer day closed its light on earth,
   And my soul grew sad with pain,
As they bore me away with oaths and mirth,
   O'er piles of the bleeding slain.

He sleeps where the blest of our glorious dead
   Were left on the sacred land;
Where the daring deeds, ere his spirit fled,
   He led with a bold command!
He sleeps—yes, he sleeps, undisturbed by war,
   Though tyrants tramp o'er his breast;
For, with those who slumber in glory afar,
   He takes an immortal rest.
     Fort Delaware.

THE RED STAIN ON THE LEAVES
By G. W. Bungay

THE wood-bird's nest upon the bough
   Deserted hangs, and heaped with leaves;
Once filled with life and joy, but now
   Sad as a stricken heart that grieves.
Amid the light of such a scene,
   Where silent vales and hills are clad
In gayest hues of gold and green,
   Why should the human heart be sad?

Yet sombre thoughts flit through the mind,
   And pass unspoken and unsung,
As leaves, touched by the autumn wind,
   Fall from the twigs to which they clung.
Here, like the patriarch in his dream,
   We see the ladder angels trod;
The mountains to our vision seem
   A footstool at the throne of God.

The veils of golden mist that rise
   Over the woodlands to the sea,
Drop where the gallant soldier lies,
   Whose furlough is eternity.
Upon the leaves now sear and red,
   That once were flakes of fire to me,
I see the blood our armies shed,
   That our dear country may be free.

FOLLOWING THE DRUM

KISS me good-by, my dear!" he said;
   "When I come back we will be wed."
Crying, she kissed him, "Good-by, Ned!"
   And the soldier followed the drum,
      The drum,
   The echoing, echoing drum.

Rataplan! Rataplan! Rataplan!
Follow me, follow me, each true man;
Living or dying, strike while you can!
  And the soldiers followed the drum,
      The drum,
  The echoing, echoing drum.

Proudly and firmly march off the men;
Who had a sweetheart thought of her then;
Tears were coming, but brave lips smiled when
  The soldiers followed the drum,
      The drum,
  The echoing, echoing drum.

One with a woman's curl next to his heart,
He felt her last smile pierce like a dart;
She thought "death in life" comes when we part
  From soldiers following the drum,
      The drum,
  The echoing, echoing drum.

THE DYING SOLDIER

WEARY and worn to a skeleton form
  He lay on a couch of pain,
And his wish at even, his prayer at morn,
  Were to visit his home again.

He talked of his mother far away,
  And he talked of his lonely wife,
When the fever frenzied his burning head
  And loosened his hold of life.

He talked of his home, the fair free land,
  The home of his childhood's play;
He talked of his babe, and the large tears fell
  And rolled from his cheeks away.

We told him his feet might never again
  Walk over his native sod,
But ere long they should tread the golden streets
  At home in the city of God.

And we said though his eye should never behold
  The forms of his earth's deep love,
He should wait for them there, by the life river fair,
  In the garden of beauty above.

But he wept, and he talked of his burial lone
  In a stranger's unnoticed bed,—
That no rose by affection's hand would be trained
  To wave o'er his grave when dead.

We told him that God would mark the spot
  Where all of his children lay,
And not one of his loved ones be forgot
  On the resurrection day.

But he sighed and whispered—"So long, so long,
  So many long weary years!
And my lonely wife and little one
  Alone in a vale of tears."

We told him the Word of God had gone forth,
  In truth and holiness,
As the Friend of the widow's lonely life,
  The Guide of the fatherless.

When death had stilled that loving heart,
  Kind hands with gentle care
Had saved for her, that lonely wife,
  One tress of his long, bright hair.

Then they wrapped the worn-out soldier's clothes
  Round the martyred hero's breast,
And in his rude, unvarnished bed,
  Laid him sadly, away to rest.

Not a hymn was sung, not a prayer was raised,
  Not a word of counsel said,
But the hireling's rude, uncareful hands
  Piled the damp mould o'er his head.

NORTHMEN, COME OUT!

DEDICATED TO THE MASSACHUSETTS REGIMENTS

BY CHARLES GODFREY LELAND

(Air—*Burschen herus!*)

NORTHMEN, come out!
Forth unto battle with storm and shout!
Freedom calls you once again,
To flag and fort and tented plain;
Then come with drum and trump and song,
And raise the war-cry wild and strong:
    Northmen, come out!

Northmen, come out!
The foe is waiting round about,
With paixhan, mortar, and petard,
To tender us their Beau-regard;
With shot and shrapnell, grape and shell.
We give them back the fire of hell;
    Northmen, come out!

Northmen, come out!
Give the pirates a roaring rout;
Out in your strength and let them know
How Working Men to Work can go.
Out in your might and let them feel
How Mudsills strike when edged with steel!
    Northmen, come out!

Northmen, come out!
Come like your grandsires stern and stout;
Though Cotton be of Kingly stock,
Yet royal heads may reach the block;
The Puritan taught it once in pain,
His sons shall teach it once again:
    Northmen, come out!

Northmen, come out!
Forth into battle with storm and shout!
He who lives with victory's blest,
He who dies gains peaceful rest.
Living or dying, let us be
Still vowed to God and Liberty!
    Northmen, come out!

OUR COUNTRY IS CALLING
By F. H. Hedge, D. D.

[Wohl auf! Cameraden! aufs Pferd, aufs Pferd.]

OUR country is calling! Go forth! go forth!
To danger and glory, ye gallants!
In danger your manhood must prove its worth,
There hearts are weighed in the balance;
And he who would win his life at last
Must throw it all on the battle's cast.

Our country is calling, our country that bleeds
With daggers that Treason has planted;
'Tis Honor that backons where Loyalty leads,
We follow with spirits undaunted.
The soldier who fronts death face to face
Is foremost now of the patriot race.

Our country is calling! we come! we come!
For Freedom and Union we rally;
Our heart-beat echoes the beating drum,
Our thoughts with the trumpet tally;
Each bosom pants for the doomful day,
When the rebels shall meet us in battle array.

Our country is calling with names that of old
Emblazoned America's story;
May those of to-day, when its tale shall be told,
Blaze with them forever in glory!
Be our banner redeemed the reward of our scars,
No scathe on its stripes and no cloud on its stars!

THE SOLDIER'S MOTHER

IT is night; almost morning—the clock has struck
    three;
Who can tell where, this moment, my darling may
    be!
On the window has gathered the moisture like dew;
I can see where the moonbeams steal tremblingly
    through;
It is cold, but not windy,—how dreary and damp
It must be for our soldiers exposed in the camp!
Though I know it is warmer and balmier there,
Yet I shrink from the thought of the chilling night
    air;
For he never was used to the hardships of men
When at home, for I shielded and cherished him then;
And to all that could tend to his comfort I saw,—
For he seemed like a child till he went to the War!

He is twenty, I know; and boys younger than he,
In the ranks going by, every day we can see;
And those stronger and prouder, by far I have met,
But I never have seen a young soldier, as yet,
With so gallant a mien, or so lofty a brow,—
How the sun and the wind must have darkened it
    now;
How he will have been changed when he comes from
    the South!—
With his beard shutting out the sweet miles of his
    mouth;
And the tremulous beauty, the womanly grace,
Will be bronzed from the delicate lines of his face,
Where, of late, only childhood's soft beauty I saw,—
For he seemed like a child till he went to the War!

He was always so gentle, and ready to yield;
And so frank, there was nothing kept back or con-
    cealed;
He was always so sparkling with laughter and joy,
I had thought he never could cease being a boy;
But when sounded the cannon for battle, and when
'Rose the rallying cry of our Nation for men,
From the dream-loving mood of his boyhood he passed;
From his path the light fetters of pleasure he cast;
And rose, ready to stand in the perilous van,

Not the tremulous boy, but the resolute man;
And I gazed on him sadly, with trembling and awe,—
He was only a child till he went to the War!

There are homes that are humbler and sadder than
    ours;
There are ways that are barer of beauty and flowers;
There are those that must suffer for fire and bread,
Living only to sorrow and wish they were dead;
I must try and be patient—I must not repine—
But what heart is more lonely, more anxious than mine!
Or what hearth can be darker than mine seems to be,
Now the glow of the firelight is all I can see,—
Where my darling, in beauty, so lately I saw,—
He was only a child, till he went to the War!

THE DEAD DRUMMER-BOY

'MIDST tangled roots that lined the wild ravine
    Where the fierce fight raged hottest through the day,
And where the dead is scattered heaps were seen,
Amid the darkling forest's shade and sheen,
        Speechless in death he lay.

The setting sun, which glanced athwart the place
    In slanting lines, like amber-tinted rain,
Fall sidewise on the drummer's upturned face,
Where death had left his gory finger's trace
        In one bright crimson stain.

The silken fringes of his once bright eye
    Lay like a shadow on his check so fair;
His lips were parted by a long-drawn sigh,
That with his soul had mounted to the sky
        On some wild martial air.

No more his hand the fierce tatoo shall beat,
    The shrill reveile, or the long roll's call,
Or sound the charge, when in the smoke and heat
Of fiery onset, foe with foe shall meet,
        And gallant men shall fall.

Yet may be in some happy home, that one,
    A mother, reading from the list of dead,
Shall chance to view the Lame of her dear son,
And move her lips to say, "God's will be done!"
    And bow in grief her head.

But more than this what tongue shall tell his story
    Perhaps his boyish longings were for fame;
He lived, he died; and so, *memento mori,*—
Enough if on the page of War and Glory
    Some hand has wrot his name.

THE SOLDIER'S "GOOD-BY"
By Mary E. Nealy

GOOD-BY, my wife, my child, my friend,
    'Tis hard to leave you all;
But there's a God in heaven above
Will bless and shield you with His love,
    If I am doomed to fall.

You know I could not stay, dear love,
    When over all the land
The shot of Sumter circled round,
And lifted, at a single bound,
    This mighty patriot-band.

A thrill that never else had swept
    Across this soul of mine,
Stirred up each tingling drop of blood,
Ready to pour a votive flood
    Upon my countriy's shrine.

O dearest! there's a manhood lies,
    Deep in these slender forms,
We know not of, till in our skies
Such clouds of danger o'er us rise
    To fill our land with storms.

Then, like a mountain stream it comes,
   A stream of power and might;
It echoes to the beat of drums,
It quails not when the fiery bombs
   Break fiercely on the sight.

This war is sad; but I thank God
   For this one blessed taste—
Of strength unknown, a mighty flood
   Which else had gone to waste.

My arms seemed braced with nerves of steel,
   My soul is firm and strong;
And, dearest, even now I feel
The power to crush beneath my heel
   The share of this foul wrong.

The man who springs not to his sword
   In such a time as this,
To see his country's fame restored,
Is weak as he who slew his Lord
   With a deceitful kiss.

Then ask me not. I cannot stay,
   My own, my blessed wife;
The God that looks on us to-day
Will listen to you when you pray,
   And shield your soldier's life.

Yet if I come not back again,
   But fall beside my foe,
This blood will not be spilled in vain
Though it should fall like crimson rain
   Where crimson waters flow.

I'm strong enough to die, dear love,
   In such a cause as ours;
For I shall see from Heaven above
Freedom's fair bow above *you wave,*
   Entwined with Freedom's powers.

Now kiss me one "good-by," my wife,
   Your task is worse than mine;
For while I revel in the strife,
You can but pray for this poor life,
   With heroism divine.

'Tis weary—all the dark suspense
  A woman has to bear:
The anguished thoughts, the woe intense
While booming cannon bear her hence
  A fear for every prayer.

But you—you must be strong and bright
  You are a soldier's wife:
I'll think of you by day and night,
Your love shall nerve me in the fight;
  Good-by, my love, my life!

THE VOLUNTEERS' WIFE TO HER HUSBAND

DON'T stop a moment to think, John,
  Your country calls—then go;
Don't think of me or the children, John,
  I'll care for them you know.
Leave the corn upon the stalk, John,
  Potatoes on the hill,
And the pumpkins on the vines, John—
  I'll gather them with a will.
But take your gun and go, John,
  Take your gun and go,
For Ruth can drive the oxen, John,
  And I can use the hoe.

I've heard my grandsire tell, John,
  (He fought at Bunker Hill,)
How he counted all his life and wealth
  His country's offering still.
Shall we shame the brave old blood, John,
  That flowed on Monmouth Plain?
No! take your gun and go, John,
  If you ne'er return again.
Then take your gun and go.

Our army's short of blankets, John,
    Then take this heavy pair;
I spun and wove them when a girl,
    And worked them with great care.
There's a rose in every corner, John,
    And there's my name you see;
On the cold ground they'll warmer feel
    That they were made by me.
Then take your gun and go.

And if it be God's will, John,
    You ne'er come back again,
I'll do my best for the children John,
    In sorrow want and pain.
In winter nights I'll teach them all
    That I have learned at school,
To love the country, keep the laws,
    Obey the Savour's rule.
Then take your gun and go.

And in the village church, John,
    And at our humble board,
We'll pray that God will keep you, John,
    And heavenly aid afford;
And all who love their country's cause
    Will love and bless you too,
And nights and mornings they will pray
    For freedom and for you.
Then take your gun and go.

And now good-by to you John—
    I cannot say farewell;
We'll hope and pray for the best, John;
    God's goodness none can tell.
Be his great arm around you John,
    To guard you night and day;
Be our beloved country's shield,
    Till the war has passed away.
Then take your gun and go.

KISS ME, MOTHER, AND LET ME GO

By Miss Nancy A. W. Priest

HAVE you heard the news that I heard to-day!
The news that trembles on every lip!
The sky is darker again, they say,
  And breakers threaten the good old ship.
Our country calls on her sons again.
  To strike in her name, at a dastard foe;
She asks for six hundred thousand men;
  I would be one, mother. Let me go.

The love of my country was born with me;
  I remember how my young heart would thrill
When I used to sit on my grandame's knee
  And list to the story of Bunker Hill.
Life gushed out there in a rich red flood;
  My grandshire fell in that fight you know;—
Would you have me shame the brave old blood!
  Nay, kiss me, mother, and let me go.

Our flag the flag of our hope and pride,
  With its stars and stripes, and its field of blue,
Is mocked, insulted, torn down, defied,
  And trampled upon by the rebel crew.
And England and France look on a sneer,
  "Ha! queen of the earth, thou art fallen low;"
Earth's downtrod millions weep and fear;
  So kiss me, mother, and let me go.

Under the burning Southern skies,
  Our brothers languish in heart-sick pain,
They turn to us with their pleading eyes;
  O mother, say, shall they turn in vain?
Their ranks are thinning from sun to sun,
  Yet bravely they hold at bay the foe;
Shall we let them die there, one by one?
  So kiss me, mother, and let me go.

Can you selfishly cling to your household joys,
  Refusing this smallest tithe to yield,
While thousands of mothers are sending boys
  Beloved as yours to the battle-field?
Can you see my country call in vain,

And restrain my arm from the needful blow?
Not so, though your heart should break with pain
You will kiss me, mother, and let me go.

A MOTHER'S ANSWER
"I HAVE KISSED HIM AND LET HIM GO"

HE'S my own boy, and this is my plea:
    Perhaps it is foolish and weak;
But mothers I'm sure will have pity on me,
    And some word will tenderly speak.
The light of my home—my tears fall like rain—
    Is it a wonder I shrink from the blow—
That my heart is crushed by its weight of pain!
    But I've kissed him, and let him go.

There are some, I know, who feel a strange pride
    In giving their country their all,—
Who count it a glory that boys from their side,
    In the strife are so ready to fall.
But I, sitting here, have no pride in my heart;
    (God forgive me that this should be so!)
For the boy that I love the tears still start,
    Yet I've kissed him, and let him go.

Last night, with soft steps, I stole to his bed
    As oft in childhood I'd done;
On his pillow I bowed my poor, stricken head
    Till out of the east rose the sun.
His dreams were of me; for he turned in his sleep,
    And murmured "Dear mother!" so low,
I bit my pale lips lest they'd cowardly speak
    "O, my darling, *I can't let you go!*"

This morning I blessed him; I stifled my pain;
    I bade him be true to his trust;
To stand by the flag till his country again
    Should raise its proud head from the dust.
I knew by the light in his beautiful eyes,—

By his face with courage aglow,—
He'd fight to the last. I choked back my sighs,
While I kissed him, and let him go.

But oh, sitting here, this desolate day,
   Still there comes no feeling of pride;
But One knows my need, and to Him will I pray,
   I can trust Him whatever betide.
And if he shall fall,—(O, faint heart, be still!)
   I knew He will soften the blow,
And I yet may feel a patriot's thrill
   That I kissed him, and let him go.

THE SOLDIER'S DREAM OF HOME
BY CAROLINE A MASON

YOU have put the children to bed, Alice,—
   Maud and Willie and Rose;—
They have lisped their sweet "Our Father,"
   And sunk to their night's repose.
Did you think of me, dear Alice?
   Did they think of me, and say,
"God bless him, and God bless him!
   Dear father far away?"

Oh, my very heart grows sick, Alice,
   I long so to behold
Rose, with her pure, white forehead,
   And Maud, with her curls of gold
And Willie, so gay and sprightly,
   So merry and full of glee;
Oh, my heart yearns to enfold ye,
   My "smiling group of three!"

I can bear the noisy day, Alice,
   The camp life, gay and wild,
Shuts from my yearning bosom
   Thoughts of wife and child:
But when the night is round me,

And under its strong beams
I gather my cloak about me,
 I dream such long, sad dreams!

I think of the pale young wife, Alice,
 who looked up in my face
When the drum beat at evening,
 And called me to my place.
I think of the three sweet birdlings
 Left in the dear home-nest
And my soul is sick with longings
 That will not be at rest.

Oh, when will the war be over, Alice!
 Oh, when shall I behold
Rose, with her pure, white forehead,
 And Maud, with her curls of gold;
And Will, so gay and sprightly,
 So merry and full of glee,
And, more than all, the dear wife
 Who bore my babes to me?

God guard and keep you all, Alice;
 God guard and keep me, too;
For if only one were missing,
 What would the other do?
Oh, when will the war be over,
 And when shall I behold
Those whom I love so dearly,
 Safe in the dear home-fold?

THE RESPONSE

I HAVE put the children to bed, Harry,—
 Rose and Willie and Maud;—
They have sung their hymns together,
 And whispered their prayer to God,

Then Rose said, gently smiling,
   "Come, Willie and Maud, now say,
God bless the dear, sweet father,—
   Father so far away!"

And such a glad trust arose, Harry,
   In this sad heart of mine,
For I felt that God would keep you
   Safe in His hand divine.
And I kissed their pure, young foreheads,
   And said, "He is over all!
He counteth the hair of your heads, darlings,
   And noteth the sparrow's fall."

Then I sung them to their sleep, Harry,
   With hymns all trust and love,
And I knew that God was listening
   From His gracious throne above.
And since that calm, sweet evening,
   I have felt so happy, dear!
And so have the children, Harry;
   They seem to know no fear.

They talk of your coming home, Harry
   As something sure to be;
I list to their childish pratings,
   Nor care to check their glee.
For oh, 'tis a cause so noble,
   And you so brave and true;
And God protects His own, Harry,
   And surely will watch o'er you.

So keep up a brave good heart, Harry!
   God willing—and He knows best—
We'll welcome you, safe and happy,
   Back to the dear home-nest.
And Maud and Rose and Willie
   Shall yet, with a moistened eye,
Give thanks to the dear good Father,
   While you stand tearful by.

GONE TO THE WAR

By Horatio Alger, Jr.

MY Charlie has gone to the war,
My Charlie so brave and tall;
He left his plough in the furrow
And flew at his country's call.
May God in safety keep him,
My precious boy—my all.

GENTLY! GENTLY!

Among the wounded was a young soldier whose
limbs were fearfully shattered. Though evidently
in intense pain, he uttered no cry; but, as the carri-
ers raised the "stretcher" he was on, he whispered,
"Gently! gently!"

Though he neither sighs nor groans,
Death is busy with his bones:
Bear him o'er the jutting stones
      Gently! gently!

Sisters, faithful to your vow
Swathe his limbs and cool his brow:
Peace! his soul is passing now
      Gently! gently!

He has fallen in the strife!
Tell it to his widowed wife,
And to her who gave him life,
      Gently! gently!

Loudly praise the brave who gem
With their blood our diadem:
And their faults—oh, speak of them
      Gently! gently!

MARCH ALONG
By George H. Boker

SOLDIERS are we from the mountain and valley,
  Soldiers are we from the hill and the plain;
Under the flag of our fathers we rally;
    Death, for its sake, is but living again
        Then march along, gay and strong,
        March to battle with a song!
        March, march, along!

We have a history told of our nation,
    We have a name that must never go down;
Heroes achieved it through toil and privation;
    Bear it on, bright with its ancient renown!
        Then march along.

Who that shall dare say the flag waving o'er us,
    Which floated in glory from Texas to Maine,
Must fall, where our ancestors bore it before us,
    Writes his own fate on the roll of the slain.
        Then march along.

Look at it, traitors, and blush to behold it!
    Quail as it flashes its stars in the sun!
Think you a hand in the nation will fold it,
    While there's a hand that can level a gun?
        Then march along.

Carry it onward till victory earn it
    The rights it once owned in the land of the free;
Then, in God's name, in our fury we'll turn it
    Full on the treachery over the sea!
        Then march along.

England shall feel what a vengeance the liar
    Stores in the bosom he aims to deceive;
England shall feel how God's truth can inspire;
    England shall feel it, but only to grieve.
        Then march along.

Peace shall unite us again and forever,
　　Though thousands lie cold in the graves of these
　　　wars;
Those who survive them shall never prove, never,
　　False to the flag of the stripes and the stars!
　　　　Then march along, gay and strong,
　　　　March to the battle with a song!
　　　　March, march along!

"THE LAST BROADSIDE"
BY ELIZABETH T. PORTER BEACH

The following lines were written upon hearing of the
heroism of the crew of the "Frigate Cumberland," in the
engagement at "Hampton Roads" who bravely fired a
last "Broadside" while their ship was sinking, in compli-
ance with the order of their Commanding Officer, the
gallant hero, Lieutenant Morris.

"SHALL WE GIVE THEM A BROADSIDE AS SHE GOES?"

SHALL we give them a Broadside, my boys, as she
　　goes!
　　Shall we send ye another to TELL,
In iron-tongued words, to Columbia's foes,
　　How bravely her sons say Farewell?

Ay! what though we sink 'neath the turbulent wave,
　　'Tis with DUTY and RIGHT at the helm;
And over the form should the fierce waters rave,
　　No tide can the spirit o'erwhelm!

For swift o'er the billows of Charon's dark stream
　　We'll pass to the Immortal shore,
Where the "waters of life" in brilliancy beam,
　　And the pure float in peace evermore!

Shall we give them a Broadside once more, my brave
 men?
 "Ay! Ay!" rose the full, earnest cry;
"A Broadside! A Broadside! we'll give them again!
 Then for God and the Right nobly die."

"Haste! Haste?"—for amid all that battling din
 Comes a gurgling sound fraught with fear,
As swift flowing waters pour rushingly in;
 Up! Up! till her portholes they near.

No blenching!—no faltering!—still fearless all seem;
 Each man firm to duty doth bide;
A flash! and a "Broadside!" a shout! a careen?
 And the Cumberland sinks 'neath the tide!

The "Star Spangled Banner" still floating above!
 As a beacon upon the dark wave!
Our Ensign of Glory, proud streaming in love,
 O'er the tomb of the "Loyal and Brave!"

Bold hearts! mighty spirits! "tried gold" of our
 land!
 A halo of glory your need!
All honored, the noble-souled Cumberland band!
 So true in Columbia's need!

THE PATRIOT GIRL TO HER LOVER
By George Vandenhoff

HARK! the trumpet is sounding, it's a war-note I
 hear;
 Arise, arm, and go forth my own Knight;
And though my hand tremble, my eye drop a tear,
 I'll gird on your sword for the fight!

O deem you the maid whose affection you claim,
 Though loving as I have loved you,

Could bear without blushing a recreant's name,
    To his country, to honor, untrue?

You have vowed that your heart and your hopes are
        in *me*,—
    That you live in the light of my eyes;
Let their lovebeam your beacon to victory be,—
    My hand of your valor the prize!

Would you win one? Be worthy of her who would
        die
    Ere be link'd to a coward or slave
And yielding her heart's blood would breathe but one
        sigh,—
    A prayer her dear country save.

Go forth then and conquer; be strong in the fight;
    Think of me, and *put heart in each blow.*
Strike for Country, for UNION, for LOVE, and for RIGHTS,
    And down with the insolent foe!

THE FALLEN SOLDIER

BEAR off your comrade, boys! See, he has fallen;
    The blow at his leader aimed, he made his own;
Loose from the bridle the stiffened hand, softly:
    Only this morning it fed his good roan.

Who knows this brave lad, for he scarce can be
        twenty,
    That just for his country was eager to die!
Just for his country, without hope of glory,
    He dropped from the saddle in darkness to lie.

Bear him in pity, and bear him in anguish;
    You think them soft lips, but they changed without
        moan;
For I, who rode next him, sprang forward and
        clasped him,
    And held both his hands, to the last, in my own.

We knew not the great heart that bore him right
    onward,
Beating its twenty good years out so well;
But, comrades, I felt the thin hands of his mother,
    Bearing up through my own when he fell.

Sad 'tis to think of the lonely brown homestead
    Set in the bleak, barren, North hills afar;
There they have loved him so, there they will mourn
    him so,
    Never returning to them from the war.

ROLL CALL
By N. G. Shepherd

"Corporal Green!" the orderly cried;
    "Here!" was the answer, loud and clear,
    From the lips of a soldier who stood near;
And "Here!" was the word the next replied.

"Cyrus Drew!"—then a silence fell;
    This time no answer followed the call;
    Only his rear-man had seen him fall,
Killed or wounded he could not tell.

There they stood in the failing light,
    These men of battle, with grave, dark looks,
    As plain to be read as open books;
While slowly gathered the shade of night.

The fern on the hill-sides were splashed with blood
    And down in the corn, where the poppies grew
    Wore redder stains than the poppies knew;
And crimson-dyed as the river's flood.

For the foe had crossed from the other side
    That day, in the face of a murderous fire
    That swept them down in its terrible ire;
And their life-blood went to color the tide.

"Herbert Cline!"—at the call there came
  Two stalwart soldiers into the line,
  Bearing between them this Herbert Cline,
Wounded and bleeding, to answer his name.

"Ezra Kerr!"—and a voice answered "Here!"
  "Hiram Kerr!" but no man replied:
  They were brothers, these two; the sad
    sighed,
And a shadow crept through the corn-field near.

"Ephraim Deane!" then a soldier spoke:
  "Deane carried our regiment's colors," he said,
  "When our ensign was shot; I left him dead,
Just after the enemy wavered and broke.

"Close to the roadside his body lies:
  I paused a moment and gave him to drink;
  He murmured his mother's name, I think;
And Death came with it and closed his eye."

"Twas a victory—yes: but it cost us dear;
  For that company, a roll, when called at night,
  Of a hundred men who went into the fight,
Numbered but twenty that answered "*Here!*"

THE UNION—RIGHT OR WRONG
By George P. Morris

I

IN Freedom's name our blades we draw,
  She arms us for the fight!
For country, government, and law,
  For Liberty and Right.
The Union must—shall be preserved,
  Our flag still o'er us fly!
That cause our hearts and hands has nerved,
  And we will do or die.

CHORUS
Then come, ye hardy volunteers,
   Around our standard throng,
And pledge man's hope of coming Years,–
   The Union,—right or wrong!
The Union,—right or wrong—inspires
   The burden of our song;
It was the glory of our sires—
   The Union—right or wrong!

II
It is the duty of us all
   To check rebellion's sway;
To rally at the nation's call,
   And we that voice obey!
Then like a band of brothers go,
   A hostile league to break,
To rout a spoil-encumbered foe,
   And what is ours retake.

CHORUS
So come, ye hardy volunteers,
   Around our standard throng,
And pledge man's hope of coming years,–
   The Union,—right or wrong!
The Union,—right or wrong-inspires
   The burden of our song!
It was the glory of our sires—
   The Union,—right or wrong!

"NEWS FROM THE WAR"

TWO women sat at a farm-house door,
   Busily reading the news,
While softly around them fair twilight sheds
   Her tender shadows and dews.

Peace smiles in the tenderest heaven above;
   Peace rests on the landscape fair;
And peace, like a holy spirit of love,
   Broods in the balmy air.

But not one ray of peace illumes
   Those sad and wistful eyes,
Which search that printed record o'er
   As mariners search the skies.

Look on their faces: one like a rose
   Fresh with the beauty of May;
The other, pale as a waning moon
   Seen through thin clouds of gray.

Yet, though one is young and the other old,
   With the same soft glory they shine;
For they're tinted with tenderest light and shadow
   By love, the artist divine.

Now fast as a radiant vision, fades
   The glow of the western skies;
Yet the readers read on,—unmindful of all
   Save the paper before their eyes.

Nothing to them the charms of that hour,—
   The magic of meadow and hill;
For spirits bowed down with a weight of care,
   Are blind to the beautiful still.

Deeper the shadows of twilight fall;
   More hushed grows the dewy air,
When suddenly breaks on that holy calm
   A quick, wild cry of despair.

The younger glances have found it first,—
   That record so sad and so brief;
"Mortally wounded!"—two dread words—
   Winged arrows of pain and grief.

"Mortally wounded!"—look again;
   Alas! it is all to true;
Not the brave alone, but the fond and fair
   Are mortally wounded, too.

He on the battle-field far away;
   They, in their quiet home,—
The wife and the mother, who never more
   Shall see their loved hero come

The grass will grow where the warrior fell,
And sweet wild flowers may bloom
On the very turf once blackened and burned
By the fearful fires of doom.

But the smiling summers, that come and go,
Can never, never heal
The bleeding bosoms which felt to-day
Something sharper than steel.

"Mortally wounded!" oh, dread War!
Many a victim is thine,
Save those who hear your terrible voice
Go thundering along the line!

If we give proud names and echoing hymns,
And build up monuments grand
To the gallant spirits who suffer and fall
In defence of their native land;

Let us yield a tenderer tribute still,—
Sad tears and a pitying sigh,—
To the uncrowned martyrs who silently sink,
And die when their heroes die.

SONG OF THE SOLDIERS
By Private Miles O'Reilly

AIR—*Jamie's on the Stormy Sea*

COMRADES known in marches many,
Comrades, tried in dangers many,
Comrades, bound by memories many,
Brothers ever let us be.
Wounds or sickness may divide us,
Marching orders may divide us,
But, whatever fate betide us,
Brothers of the heart are we.

Comrades, known by faith the clearest,
Tried when death was near and nearest,
Bound we are by ties the dearest,
      Brothers evermore to be.
And, if spared, and growing older.
Shoulder still in line with shoulder,
And with hearts no thrill the colder,
      Brothers ever we shall be.

By communion of the banner,—
Crimson, white, and starry banner,—
By the baptism of the banner,
      Children of one Church are we.
Creed nor faction can divide us,
Race nor language can divide us,
Still whatever fate betide us,
      Children of the Flag are we!

OUR UNION AND OUR FLAG
By Ruth N. Cromwell

MY flag, when first those starry folds
    Which waved o'er Sumter's band
Received the traitor's murderous fire,
    How flashed the tumult through the land.
No soul e'er panted for the hour
    That lifts it from love's torturing rack
As panted, then, a nation's heart
    To hurl the insult back.

If shame then hushed Columbia's breath
    And bowed her beauteous form,
'Twas but the siroc's awful pause,—
    The lull before the storm
Then men awoke, soul spoke to soul,
    And hand grasped hand, for woe or weal;
Then wavering hearts were turned to iron,
    And nerves were turned to steel.

Old feuds were not, old parties died;
    From vale to mountain crag,
A nation's shout linked friend and foe
    Our Union and our flag;
We gave our men as freely then
    As leaves from forest tree;
We gave our gold, as rivers give
    their waters to the sea.

Still floats on high Columbia's flag,
    In the gloom of autumn day,—
The blot still on her starry folds,
    The stain not washed away;
For Moultrie stands, and Charleston lives,
    And Freedom's sun grows pale;
Oh! God, whate'er thy children's doom,
    Let not her foes prevail.

We point to Ellsworth's honored tomb,
    To Lyon's fall, to Baker's grave;
What say Missouri's vine-clad hills?
    What answer from Potomac's wave?
What answer they? Men ask of men
    Who never yet foreswore the vow;
What answer they? the nation asks,
    With lowering heart and brow.

Men, whom Columbia's voice hath call'd
    To guide the ship of State,
Remember well each soul on board
    Owns portion in her freight;
More clean was Nero's recking brow,
    More guiltless Arnold's past,
Than the hand that falters at the helm,
    Or shrinks before the blast.

THE TWO FURROWS
By C. H. Webb

THE spring-time came—but not with mirth—
The banner of our trust,
And with it the best hopes of earth,
Were trailing in the dust.

The Farmer saw the shame from far,
And stopped his plough afield:
"Not the blade of peace but the brand of war
This arm of mine must wield.

"When traitor hands that flag would stain,
Their homes let women keep;
Until its stars burn bright again,
Let others sow and reap."

The Farmer sighed,—"A lifetime long
The plough has been my trust;
In truth it were an arrant wrong
To leave it now to rust."

With ready strength the Farmer tore
The iron from the wood,
And to the village smith he bore
That ploughshare stout and good.

The blacksmith's arms were bare and brown,
And loud the bellows roared;
The Farmer flung his ploughshare down,—
"Now forge me out a sword!"

And then a merry, merry chime,
The sounding anvil rung,—
Good sooth, it was a nobler rhyme
Than ever poet sung.

The blacksmith wrought with skill that day,
The blade was keen and bright;
And now where thickest is the fray
The Farmer leads the fight.

Not as of old that blade he sways
  To break the meadow's sleep,
But through the rebel ranks he lays
  A furrow broad and deep.

The Farmer's face is burned and brown,
  But light is on his brow;
Right well he wots what blessings crown
  The furrow of the Plough.

"But better is to-days success,"—
  Thus ran the Farmer's word,—
"For nations yet unborn shall bless
  This furrow of the Sword."

SHALL FREEDOM DROOP AND DIE!
By Charles G. Leland

SHALL Freedom droop and die,
  And we stand idle by,
When countless millions yet unborn
  Will ask the reason why!

If for her flag on high
  You bravely fight and die,
Be sure that God on his great roll
  Will mark the reason why.

But should ye basely fly,
  Scared by the battle-cry,
Then down through all eternity
  You'll hear the reason why.

THE PICKET GUARD

"ALL quiet along the Potomac," they say,
  "Except now and then a stray picket
Is shot, as he walks on his beat, to and fro,
  By a rifleman hid in the thicket.
'Tis nothing—a private or two, now and then;
  Will not count in the news of the battle;
Not an officer lost—only one of the men,
  Moaning out, all alone, the death-rattle."

All quiet along the Potomac to-night,
  Where the soldiers lie peacefully dreaming
Their tents, in the rays of the clear autumn moon,
  Or the light of the watch-fires are gleaming.
A tremulous sigh, as the gently night-wind
  Through the forest leaves softly is creeping;
While stars up above, with their glittering eyes
  Keep guard—for the army is sleeping.

There's only the sound of the lone sentry's tread
  As he tramps from the rock to the fountain,
And thinks of the two in the low trundle-bed,
  Far away in the cot on the mountain.
His musket falls slack,—his face, dark and grim,
  Grows gentle with memories tender,
As he mutters a prayer for the children asleep,—
  For their mother,—may Heaven defend her!

The moon seems to shine just as brightly as then,
  That night, when the love yet unspoken
Leaped up to his lips,—when low, murmured vows
  Were pledged to be ever unbroken.
Then draping his sleeve roughly over his eyes,
  He dashes off tears that are welling,
And gathers his gun closer up to its place,
  As if to keep down the heart-swelling

He passes the fountain, the blasted pine-tree—
  The footstep is lagging and weary;
Yet onward he goes, through the broad belt of light,
  Toward the shades of the forest so dreary,
Hark! was it the night-wind that rustled the leaves!
  Was it moonlight so wondrously flashing?
It looked like a rifle—"Ha! Mary, good-by!"
  And the life-blood is ebbing and plashing,

All quiet along the Potomac to-night,—
No sound save the rush of the river;
While soft falls the dew on the face of the dead,—
The picket's off duty forever.

TO THE MEN OF THE NORTH AND WEST
By R. H. Stoddard

MEN of the North and West,
　Wake in your might,
Prepare, as the rebels have done.
　For the fight!
You cannot shrink from the test,
Rise! Men of the North and West!

They have torn down your banner of stars;
　They have trampled the laws;
They have stifled the freedom they hate,
　For no cause!
Do you love it or slavery best?
Speak! Men of the North and West.

They strike at the life of the State:—
　Shall the murder be done?
They cry, "We are two!" And you?
　"We are one!"
You must meet them, then, breast to breast
On! Men of the North and West!

Not with words; they laugh them to scorn,
　And tears they despise;
But with swords in your hands, and death
　In your eyes!
Strike home! leave to God all the rest.
Strike! Men or the North and West!

ACROSS THE LINES
By Ethel Lynn

LEFT for dead? I—Charlie Coleman,
  On the field we won—and lost,
Like a dog; the ditch my death-bed
  My pillow but a log across.
Helpless hangs my arm beside me,
  Drooping lies my aching head;
How strange it sounded when that soldier,
  Passing, spoke of me as "dead."

Dead? and here—where yonder banner
  Flaunts its scanty group of stars,
And that rebel emblem binds me
  Close within those bloody bars.
Dead? without a stone to tell it,
  Nor a flower above my breast!
Dead? where none will whisper softly,
  "Here a brave man lies at rest!"

Help me, Thou, my mother's helper,—
  Jesus, Thou who biding here,
Loved like me an earthly mother,
  Be thou still to aid me near.
Give me strength to totter yonder,
  Hold me up till o'er me shines
The flag of Union—there she promised
  To meet me, just beyond the lines.

Well I know how she will wander
  Where a woman's foot may stray,
Looking with those eyes so tender
  Where the poor boys wounded lay.
How her hand will bring them water,
  For her own boy Charlie's sake,
And when dying bid them whisper,
  "I pray the Lord my soul to take."

Ah! I stand on foot but feebly,
  And the blood runs very fast,
Yet by fence and bush I'll stagger
  Till the rebel lines be past.
"Courage, Charlie! twist it tighter,—

The tourniquet about your arm;
Be a man—don't faint and shiver
    When the lifetide trickles warm."

Faint and weak,—still coming, mother,
    Walking some, but creeping more,
Fearing lest the watchful sentry
    Stops the heart-beat,—slow before
Stay—with fingers ruddy dabbled
    Loose the belt your waist confines;
Write upon it "Charlie Coleman—
    Carry him across the lines."

Trembling letters—but some stranger
    Chance may read them when I'm gone,
And for the sake of love and pity
    Bear my lifeless body on.
Coming! ah—what means this darkness—
    Night too soon is coming on.
Mother, are you waiting?—"Jesus,
    Tell her that with You I've gone."

Then the head her heart had pillowed,
    Drooping laid it down to rest,
As calm as when in baby slumber
    Its locks were cradled on her breast.

            *   *   *   *   *   *   *

Glowed the sunset o'er the meadow,
    Lighting up the gloomy pines,
Where a body only lingered—
    Charlie's soul had crossed the lines.

A passing soldier—foe, yet human—
    Stooped to read the words of blood;
So pitiful, so sadly earnest;
    And bore him onward through the wood.

Beneath the white flag bore him safely.
    Now, while Indian Summer shines,
A mothers's tears dew springing myrtle,
    O'er Charlie's grave across the lines.

THE CAPTAIN'S WIFE
BY THEODORE TILTON

WE gathered roses, Blanche and I, for little Madge
  one morning;
"Like every soldier's wife," said Blanche, "I dread a
  soldier's fate."
Her voice a little trembled then, as under some fore-
  warning.
A soldier galloped up the lane, and halted at the gate.

"Which house is Malcolm Blake's?" he cried; "A
  letter for his sister!"
And when I thanked him, Blanche inquired, "But
  none for me, his wife?"
The soldier played with Madge's curls, and, stooping
  over, kissed her:
"Your father was my captain, child!—I loved him as
  my life!"

Then suddenly he galloped off and left the rest unspoken.
I burst the seal, and Blanche exclaimed,—"What
  makes you tremble so?"
What answer did I dare to speak? How ought the
  news be broken?
I could not shield her from the stroke, yet tried to
  ease the blow.

"A battle in the swamps," I said; "our men were
  brave, but lost it."
And, pausing there.—"The note," I said, "is not in
  Malcolm's hand."
And first a flush flamed through her face, and then a
  shadow crossed it.
"Read quick, dear May!—read all, I pray—and let me
  understand!"

I did not read it as it stood,—but tempered so the
  phrases
As not at first to hint the worst,—held back the fatal
  word,
And half retold his gallant charge, his shout, his comrades' praises—
Till like a statue carved in stone, she neither spoke
  nor stirred!

Oh, never yet a woman's heart was frozen so com-
pletely!
So unbaptized with helping tears!—so passionless and
dumb!
Spellbound she stood, and motionless,—till little
Madge spoke sweetly:
"Dear mother, is the battle done! and will my father
come?"

I laid my finger on her lips, and set the child to playing.
Poor Blanche! the winter in her cheek was snowy like
her name!
What could she do but kneel and pray,—and linger after
her praying?
O Christ! when other heroes die, moan other wives
the same?

Must other women's hearts yet break, to keep the
Cause from failing?
God pity our brave lovers then, who face the battle's
blaze?
And pity wives in widowhood!—But is it unavailing?
O Lord! give Freedom first, then Peace!—and unto
Thee be praise!

MOVE ON THE COLUMNS
By W. D. Gallagher.

I.

MOVE on the columns! Why delay?
  Our soldiers sicken in their camps:
The summer heats, the autumn damps,
  Have sapp'd their vigor, day by day
And now the winter comes apace,
  With death-chills in its cold embrace,
More fatal than the battle fray.

II.

Move on the columns! Hesitate
   No longer what to plan or do:
Our cause is good—our men are true—
   This fight is for the Flag, the State,
The Union, and the hope of man:
   And Right will end what Wrong began,
For God the Right will vindicate.

III.

Move on the columns! If the land
   Is lock'd by winter, take the sea;
No possible barrier can be
   So fatal to a rightful stand,
As wavering purpose when at bay.
   This or THAT—"at once! to-day!"
Where worth ten thousand men at hand.

IV.

Move on the columns! With the sweep
   Of eagles let them strike the foe;
The hurricane lays the forest low:
   Momentum wings the daring leap
That clears the chasm: the lightning stroke
   Shivers the wind-defying oak;
The earthquake rocks the eternal steep,

V.

Move on the columns! Why have sprung
   Our myriad hosts from hill and plain?
Leaving the sickle in the grain,—
   Closing the harvest hymn half sung,—
Half filled the granary and the mow,—
   Unturn'd the sod, untouch'd the plough,—
Scythes rusting where they last were hung.

VI.

Move on the columns! They are here
   To found anew a people's faith,
To save from treason and from death
   A nation which they all revere;
And on each manly brow is set
   A purpose such as never yet
Was thwarted when, as now, sincere.

VII.

Move on the columns! Earth contains
    No guerdon for the good and free
Like that which bless'd our Liberty:
    And while its banner still remains
The symbol of united power,
    Nor man nor fiend can tell the hour
In which its star-lit glory wanes.

VIII.

Move on the columns strong and bright!
    Strike down the sacrilegious hands
That clutch and wield the battle brands
    Which menace with their Wrong our Right,
Words now are wasted—glittering steel
    Alone can make the last appeal:
They've wil'd it so—and we must fight.

IX.

Move on the columns! If they go
    By ways they had not thought to take
To fields we had not meant to make;
    Or if they bring unthought-of woe,
Let that which woke the fiery wrath
    Fall scorn'd and blackening in its path.
    Not man, but God, may stay the blow.
    Move on the columns!

THE SOLDIER'S SWEETHEART
BY GEORGE W. BUNGAY

I GO down to the sea,
    Where the waves speak to me
Of my darling, the soul of my soul;
    But her footprints no more
    Mark the desolate shore,
Where she tempted the billows to roll.

There the sad billows break,
    Like my heart for her sake,
On the lonely and desolate shore;

For the waves of the sea
Are now sighing with me,
For a mortal, now mortal no more.

With my heart filled with tears
And my hopes chilled with fears,
By the grave of my darling I knelt;
And I uttered a prayer
On the listening air,
Whose dew wept the sorrow I felt.

There the winds wove a shroud
Of a dim passing cloud,
Betwixt me and the bright stars above;
And the form in its fold,
Like the shape under mould,
Was the form of the angel I love.

Would that I were a flower,
Born of sunshine and shower;
I would grow on the grave of the dead.
I would sweeten the air
With the perfume of prayer,
Till my soul with its incense had fled

And I never would fade
In the delicate shade
Of the tree in whose shadow she lies.
There my petals should bloom,
By her white rural tomb.
When the stars closed their beautiful eyes

Now I see her in dreams
On the banks of the streams,
In the dear land of exquisite bliss,
Where the sweep of her wings,
And the song that she sings,
Oft awake me to sadness in this.

CARTE DE VISITE

"TWAS a terrible fight," the soldier said!
"Our Colonel was one of the first to fall,
Shot dead on the field by a rifle ball,—
A braver heart than his never bled."

A group for the painter's art were they;
The soldier with scarred and sunburnt face,
A fair-haired girl' full of youth and grace,
And her aged mother, wrinkled and gray.

These three in porch, where the sunlight came
Through the tangled leaves of the jasmine-vine,
Spilling itself like a golden wine.
And flecking the doorway with rings of flame.

The soldier had stopped to rest by the way,
For the air was sultry with summer-heat;
The road was like ashes under the feet,
And a weary distance before him lay.

"Yes, a terrible fight; our Ensign was shot
As the order to charge was given the men;
When one from the ranks seized our colors, and
then
He, too, fell dead on the self-same spot.

"A handsome boy was this last: his hair
Clustered in curls round his noble brow;
I can almost fancy I see him now,
With the scarlet stain on his face so fair.

What was his name?—have you never heard?—
Where was he from, this youth who fell?
And your regiment, stranger, which was it?
"Our regiment? It was the Twenty-third"

The color fled from the young girl's cheek,
Leaving it as white as the face of the dead;
The mother lifted her eyes and said:
"Pity my daughter—in mercy speak!"

"I never knew aught of this gallant youth,"
  The soldier answered; not even his name,
Or from what part of our State he came:—
As God is above, I speak the truth!

"But when we buried our dead that night,
  I took from his breast this picture,—see!
It is as like him as like can be:
Hold it this way, toward the light."

THE BATTLE SUMMER
BY HENRY T. TUCKERMAN

THE summer wanes,—her languid sighs now yield
  To autumn's cheering air;
The teeming orchard and the waving field
  Fruition's glory wear.

More clear against the flushed horizen wall,
  Stand forth each rock and tree;
More near the cricket's note, the plover's call
  More chrystalline the sea.

The sunshine chastened, like a mother's gaze,
  The meadow's vagrant balm;
The purple leaf and amber-tinted maize
  Reprove us while they calm.

For on the landscape's brightly pensive face,
  War's angry shadow lie;
His ruddy stains upon the woods we trace,
  And in the crimson sky

No more we bask in Earth's contented smile,
  But sternly muse apart;
Vainly her charms the patriot's soul beguile
  Or woo the orphan's heart.

Yon keen-eyed stars with mute reproaches brand
  The lapse from faith and law,—
No more harmonious emblems of a land
  Ensphered in love and awe.

As cradled in the noontide's warm embrace,
  And bathed in dew and rain,
The herbage freshened, and in billowy grace
  Wide surged the ripening grain;

And the wild rose and clover's honeyed cell
  Exhaled their peaceful breath,
On the soft air broke Treason's fiendish yell—
  The harbinger of death!

Nor to the camp alone his summons came
  To blast the glowing day.
But heavenward bore upon the wings of flame
  Our poet's mate away;*

And set his seal upon the statesman's lips
  On which a nation hung;†
And rapt the noblest life in cold eclipse,
  By woman lived or sung.‡

How shrinks the heart from Nature's festal noon,
  As shrink the withered leaves,—
In the wan light of Sorrow's harvest moon
  To glean her blighted sheaves.

*Mrs. Longfellow.   †Cavour.   ‡Mrs. Browning

A RAINY DAY IN CAMP
By Mrs. Robert Shaw Howland

IT'S a cheerless, lonesome evening,
  When the soaking, sodden ground
Will not echo to the footfall
  Of the sentinel's dull round.

God's blue star-spangled banner
    To-night is not unfurled,
Surely *He* has not deserted
    This weary, warring world.

I peer into the darkness,
    And the crowding fancies come;
The night-wind. blowing Northward
    Carries all my heart toward home.

For I listed in this army
    Nor exactly to my mind;
But my country called for helpers,
    And I couldn't stay behind.

So, I've had a sight of drilling,
    And have roughed it many ways,
And Death has nearly had me;
    Yet I think the service pays.

It's a blessed sort of feeling,
    Whether you live or die;
You helped her country in her need,
    And fought right loyally

But I can't help thinking, sometimes,
    When a wet day's leisure comes,
That I hear the old home voices
    Talking louder than the drums,

And the far, familiar faces,
    Peep in at the tent door,
And the little children's footsteps
    Go pit-pat on the floor,

I can't help thinking, somehow,
    Of all the parson reads
About that other soldier-life
    Which every true man leads.

And wife, soft-hearted creature,
    Seems a-saying in my ear,
"I'd rather have you in *those* ranks
    Than to see you Brigadier."

I call myself a brave one,
  But in my heart I lie!
For my Country and her Honor
  I am fiercely free to die.

But when the Lord who bought me,
  Asks for my service here,
To "fight the good fight" faithfully,
  I'm skulking in the rear.

And yet I know this Captain
  All love and care to be;
He would never get impatient
  With a raw recruit like me.

And I know He'd not forget me,
  When the Day of Peace appears;
I should share with Him the victory
  Of all his volunteers.

And it's kind of cheerful, thinking
  Beside the dull tent fire,
About that big promotion
  When He says, "Come up higher."

And though it's dismal rainy,
  Even now, with thoughts of Him,
Camp-life looks extra cheery,
  And death a deal less grim.

For I seem to see Him waiting
  Where a gathered Heaven greets
A great, victorious army,
  Surging up the golden streets;

And I hear Him read the roll-call
  And my heat is all aflame,
  When the dear, Recording Angel
  Writes down my happy name!

But my fire is dead white ashes,
  And the tent is chilling cold,
And I'm playing *win the battle*,
  When I've never been enrolled.

THE CAVALRY CHARGE
By Francis A. Durvage

WITH bray of the trumpet
And roll of the drum,
And keen ring of bugle,
The cavalry come.
Sharp clank the steel scabbards,
The bridle-chains ring,
And foam from red nostrils
The wild chargers fling.

Tramp! tramp! o'er the greensward
That quivers below,
Scarce held by the curb-bit
The fierce horses go!
And the grim-visaged colonel,
With ear-rending shout,
Peals forth to the squadrons
The order—"trot out!"

One hand on the sabre,
And one on the rein,
The troopers move forward
In line on the plain.
As rings the word "Gallop!"
The steel scabbards clank,
And each rowel is pressed
To a horse's hot flank;
And swift is their rush
As the wild torrents flow,
When it pours from the crag
On the valley below.

"Charge!" thunders the leader:
Like shaft from the bow
Each mad horse is hurled
On the wavering foe.
A thousand bright sabres
Are gleaming in air;
A thousand dark horses
Are flashed on the square.

Resistless and reckless
    Of aught may betide,
Like demons, not mortals,
    The wild troopers ride.
Cut right! and cut left!—
    For the parry who needs!
The bayonets shiver
    Like wind-shattered reeds.
Vain—vain the red volley
    That bursts from the square,
The random-shot bullets
    Are wasted in air.
Triumphant, remorseless,
    Unerring as death,—
No sabre that's stainless
    Returns to its sheath.

The wounds that are dealt
    By that murderous steel
Will never yield case
    For the surgeon to heal.
Hurrah! they are broken—
    Hurrah! boys, they fly—
None linger save those
    Who but linger to die.

Rein up your hot horses
    And call in your men,—
The trumpet sounds "Rally
    To color" again.
Some saddles are empty,
    Some comrades are slain,

And some noble horses
    Lie stark on the plain,
But war's a chance game, boys,
    And weeping is vain.

LYON

SING, bird, on green Missouri's plain,
  The saddest song of sorrow;
Drop tears, O clouds, in gentlest rain
  Ye from the winds can borrow;
Breathe out, ye winds, your softest sigh,
  Weep flowers, in dewy splendor,
For him who knew well how to die,
  But never to surrender.

Up rose serene the August sun,
  Upon that day of glory;
Up curled from musket and from gun
  The war-cloud gray and hoary;
It gathered like a funeral pall,
  Now broken and now blended,
Where rang the buffalo's angry call,
  And rank with rank contended.

Four thousand men, as brave and true
  As e'er went forth in daring,
Upon the foe that morning threw
  The strength of their despairing.
They feared not death,—men bless the field
  That patriot soldiers die on;
Fair Freedom's cause was sword and shield,—
  And at their head was Lyon!

Their leader's troubled soul looked forth
  From eyes of troubled brightness;
Sad soul! the burden of the North
  Had pressed out all its lightness.
He gazed upon the unequal fight,
  His ranks all rent and gory,
And felt the shadows close like night
  Round his career of glory.

"General, come, lead us!" loud the cry
  From a brave band was ringing—
"Lead us, and we will stop, or die,
  That battery's awful singing."
He spurred to where his heroes stood,
  Twice wounded,—no wound knowing,—
The fire of battle in his blood
  And on his forehead glowing.

Oh, cursed for aye that traitor's hand,
  And cursed that aim so deadly,
Which smote the bravest of the land,
  And dyed his bosom redly!
Serene he lay while past him pressed
  The battle's furious billow,
As calmly as a babe may rest
  Upon its mother's pillow.

So Lyon died! and well may flowers
  His place of burial cover,
For never had this land of ours
  A more devoted lover.
Living his country was his pride,
  His life he gave her dying,—
Life, fortune, love,—he naught denied
  To her and to her sighing.

Rest, Patriot, in thy hill-side grave,
  Beside her form who bore thee!
Long may the land thou died'st to save
  Her bannered stars wave o'er thee!
Upon her history's brightest page,
  And on Fame's glowing portal,
She'll writ thy grand, heroic page,
  And grave thy name immortal!

MARCH!

By Bayard Taylor

WITH rushing winds and gloomy skies
  The dark and stubborn Winter dies;
Far off, unseen, Spring faintly cries,
Bidding her earliest child arise:
          March!

By streams still held in icy snare,
On Southern hill-sides, melting bare,

O'er fields that motley colors wear,
That summons fills the changeful air;
                    March!

What though conflicting seasons make
Thy days their field, they woo or shake
The sleeping lids of life awake,
And Hope is stronger for thy sake:
                    March!

Then from the mountains, ribbed with snow,
Once more thy rousing bugle blow,
And East and West, and to and fro,
Proclaim thy coming to the foe:
                    March!

Say to the picket, chilled and numb,
Say to the camp's impatient hum,
Say to the trumpet and the drum:
Lift up your hearts, I come, I come!
                    March!

Cry to the waiting hoast that stray
On sandy sea-sides far away,
By marshy isle and gleaming bay,
Where Southern March is Norther May:
                    March!

Announce thyself with welcome noise,
Where Glory's victor-eagles poise
Above the proud, heroic boys
Of Iowa and Illinois:
                    March!

Then down the long Potomac's line
Shout like a storm on hills of pine,
Till ramrods ring and bayonets shine,—
"Advance! the Chieftain's call is mine:
                    "March!"

ON GUARD

By John G. Nicolay

IN the black terror-night,
  On yon mist-shrouded hill,
Slowly, with footstep light,
  Stealthy and grim and still,
Like ghost in winding sheet
  Risen at midnight bell,
Over his lonely beat
  Marches the sentinel!

In storm-defying cloak—
  Hand on his trusty gun—
Heart, like a heart of oak—
  Eye, never-setting sun;
Speaks but the challenge-shout.
  All foes without the line,
Heeds but, to solve the doubt,
  Watchword and countersign.

Camp-ward the watchfires gleam
  Beacon-like in the gloom;
Round them his comrades dream
  Pictures of youth and home.
While in his heart the bright
  Hope-fires shine everywhere,
In love's enchanting light
  Memory lies dreaming there.

Faint, through the silence come
  From the foes' grim array,
Growl of impatient drum
  Eager for morrow's fray,
Echo of song and shout,
  Curse the carousal glee,
As in a fiendish rout
  Demons at revelry.

Close, in the gloomy shade—
  Danger lurks ever nigh—
Grasping his dagger-blade
  Crouches th' assassin spy;

Shrinks at the guardsman's tread
Quails 'fore his gleaming eyes,
Creeps back with baffled hate,
Cursing his cowardice.

Naught can beguile his bold,
Unsleeping vigilance;
E'en in the fireflame, old
Visions unheeded dance.
Fearless of lurking spy,
Scornful of wassail-swell,
With an undaunted eye
Marches the sentinel.

Low, to his trusty gun
Eagerly whispers he,
"Wait, with the morning sun
March we to victory,
Fools, into Satan's clutch
Leaping ere dawn of day:
He who would fight must watch,
He who would win must pray,"

Pray! for the night hath wings;
Watch! for the foe is near;
March! till the morning brings
Fame-wreath or soldier's bier.
So shall the poet write,
When all hath ended well,
"Thus through the nation's night
Marched Freedom's sentinel."

COMING HOME

They are coming home, coming home—
Brother and lover, father and son,
Friend and foe,—they are coming home
To rest, for their work is done.

They come from the hospital, picket and field,—
From iron boat and frowning fort,—
In silent companies, slowly wheeled,
In the rhythm of a doleful thought.

This was a father of women and men,
Gray-haired, but hale, and strong of limb;
The bayonet flashed and flashed again,
And the old man's eyes grew dim.

Here was a form of manly grace;
The bomb-shell groaning through the air
Drenched with his blood a pictured face
and a curl of silken hair.

This was a bright-eyed, venturesome boy;
Back from the perilous picket-ground
They bore him, waked from his dream of joy
To a ghastly, fatal wound.

And thus for three days lingering,
He talked in wandering, rapid speech,
Of mother and home, and the cooling spring
His lips could almost reach.

They are coming home: but not as they went,
With the flying flag and stirring band;
With the tender word and message sent
From the distant waving hand.

AFTER ALL
By William Winter

THE apples are ripe in the orchard,
The work of the reaper is done,
And the golden woodlands redden
In the blood of the dying sun.

At the cottage-door the grandsire
Sits pale in his easy-chair,

While the gentle wind of twilight
Plays with his silver hair.

A woman is kneeling beside him;
A fair young head is pressed,
In the first wild passion of sorrow,
Against his aged breast.

And far from over the distance
The faltering echoes come
Of the dying blast of trumpet,
And the rattling roll of drum.

And the grandsire speaks in a whispering:
"The end no man can see;
But we give him to his country,
And we give our prayers to Thee."

The violets star the meadows,
The rose-buds fringe the door,
And over the grassy orchard
The pink-white blossoms pour.

But the grandsire's chair is empty,
The cottage is dark and still;
There's a nameless grave in the battle-field,
And a new one under the hill.

And pallid, tearless woman
By the cold hearth sits alone,
And the old clock in the corner
Ticks on with a steady drone.

BALLADS

of

THE SOUTH

Ballads of the War

SOUTHERN SONG OF FREEDOM
AIR—"THE MINSTREL'S RETURN"

A nation has sprung into life
  Beneath the bright Cross of the South;
And now a loud call to the strife
  Rings out from the shrill bugle's mouth.
They gather from morass and mountain,
  They gather from prairie and mart,
To drink at young Liberty's fountain,
  The nectar that kindles the heart.
    Then, hail to the land of the pine!
    The home of the noble and free;
    A palmetto wreath we'll entwine
    Round the altar of young Liberty!

Our flag, with its cluster of stars,
  Firm fixed in a field of pure blue,
All shining through red and white bars,
  Now gallantly flutters in view.
The stalwart and brave round it rally,
  They press to their lips every fold,
While the hymn swells from hill and from valley,
  "Be God with our Volunteers bold."
    Then, hail to the land of the pine!

Th' invaders rush down from the North,
    Our borders are black with their hordes;
Like wolves for their victims they flock,
    While whetting their knives and their sword
Their watchword is "Booty and Beauty,"
    Their aim is to steal as they go;
But, Southrons, act up to your duty,
    And lay the foul miscreants low.
        Then, hail to the laud of the pine!

The God of our fathers looks down
    And blesses the cause of the just;
His smile will the patriot crown
    Who tramples his chains in the dust.
March, march Southrons! shoulder to shoulder,
    One heart-throb, one shout for the cause;
Remember—the world's a beholder,
    And your bayonets are fixed at your doors!
        Then, hail to the land of the pine!
        The home of the noble and free;
    A palmetto wreath we'll entwine
    Round the altar of Liberty.

J. H. M.

WHAT THE SOUTH WINDS SAY

Faint as the echo of an echo born,
A bugle-note swells on the air;
Now louder, fuller, far and near,
    It sounds a mighty horn.

The noblest blast blown in our time
Comes from the South on every breeze,
To sweep across the shining seas
    In sympathy sublime!

'Tis Freedom's *reveille* that comes
Upon the air' blent with a tramp,
Which tells that she now seats her camp,
    With trumpets and with drums.

When first I heard that pealing horn,
Its sounds were faint and black int he night;
But soon I saw a burst of light
    That told of coming morn!

When first I heard that martial trend,
Swell on the chilly morning breeze,
'Twas faint as sound of distant seas,—
    Now, it might rouse the dead!

Aye, it has roused the dead! They start
From many a battle-field to teach
Their children noble thoughts and speech—
    To "fire the Southern heart!"

Not only noble thoughts, but deeds,
Our fathers taught us how to dare;
They fling our banners on the air,
    And bring our battle-steeds!

While louder rings that mighty horn,
Whose clarion notes on every gale
Tells history's latest, greatest tale—
    A nation now is born!

And at that trump's inspiring peal,
Within Time's lists I see it stand,
A splendid banner in its hand,
    Full armed from head to heel!

Long ages in their flight shall see
That flag wave o'er a nation brave—
A people who preferred one grave
    Sooner than slavery!

THE BATTLE OF BETHEL CHURCH
JUNE 10, 1861

As hurtles the tempest,
  Proclaiming the storm,
The Northern invaders
  Tumultuously swarm.
Loudly rings their battle-cry,
Glares with fury every eye;
Virginia's sons they swear shall die,
Or wear their chains of slavery.

As meets the chafed ocean
  The immutable rock,
The brave Southern freemen
  Await the stern shock.
Firm is every lip compressed,
Front to foe is every breast,
While silent prayer to Heaven attest
  Resolve for death or victory.

They number by thousands,
  The men that assail;
The hundreds that wait them,
  Oh! can they prevail?
Spoils and beauty urge the fray,
Hearts and homes contest the day,
And fiercely brands the battle's bray,
  While Right and Might strive valiantly.

Down sweet the invaders,
  Like billows of storm,—
Dead, wounded, and dying,
  They backward are borne.
Vain they rally, vain return,—
Lead and steel and graves they earn;
While angels guard their ranks from harm
  Who fight for homes and liberty.

See! see! they are flying!
  Quick, up and pursue!
And mete out the measure
  The hirelings due!

Wolves, as brave, to sheepfolds hie;
Lambs, less swift, from lions fly;
While thanks, ascend to Him on high
Who gave our arms the victory.

GOD SAVE THE SOUTH!
BY R. S. A.

Wake, every minstrel strain!
    Ring o'er each Southern plain—
God save the South!
Still let this noble band,
Joined now in heart and hand,
Fight for our sunny land,—
    Land of the South.

Armed in such sacred cause,
We covet no vain applause;
    Our swords are free.
No spot of wrong of shame
Rests on our banner's fame,
Flung forth in Freedom's name
    O'er mound and sea.

Then let the invader come;
Soon will the beat of drum
    Rally us all.
Forth from our homes we go—
Death! death! to every foe;
Says each maiden low:
    God save us all!

Ay, when the battle-hour
Darkest may seem to lower,
    God is our trust.

THE SOUTH IN ARMS
By Rev. J. H. Martin

Oh! see ye not the sight sublime,
   Unequalled in all previous time,
Presented in this Southern clime,
   The home of chivalry?

A warlike race of freemen stand,
With martial front and sword in hand,
Defenders of their native land,—
   The sons of Liberty.

Unawed by numbers, they defy
The tyrant North, nor will they fly
Resolved to conquer or to die,
   And win a glorious name.

Sprung from renowned heroic sires,
Inflamed with patriotic fires,
Their bosoms burn with fierce desires,
   The thirst for victory.

'Tis not the love of bloody strife,
The horrid sacrifice of life,
But thoughts of mother, sister, wife,
   That stir their manly heart.

A sense of honor bids them go,
To meet a hireling, ruthless foe,
And deal in wrath the deadly blow
   Which vengence loud demands.

In Freedom's sacred cause they fight,
For Independence, Justice,
And to resist a desperate might.
And by Manassas' glorious name,
And by Missouri's fields of fame,
We hear them swear, with one acclaim,
   We'll triumph, or we'll die!

"CALL ALL! CALL ALL!"
By "Georgia"

Whoop! the Doodles have broken loose,
Roaring round like the very deuce!
Lice of Egypt, a hungry pack,—
After 'em, boys, and drive 'em back.

Bull-dog, terrior, cur, and fice,
Back to the beggarly land of ice;
Worry 'em, bite 'em, scratch and tear
Everybody and everywhere.

Old Kentucky is caved from under,
Tennessee is split assunder,
Alabama awaits attack,
And Georgia bristles up her back.

Old John Brown is dead and gone!
Still his spirit is marching on,—
Lantern-jawed, and legs, my boys,
Long as an ape's from Illinois!

Want a weapon? Gather a brick,
Club or cudgel, or stone or stick;
Anything with a blade or butt,
Anything that can cleave or cut.

Anything heavy, or hard, or keen!
Any sort slaying machine!
Anything with a willing mind.
And the steady arm of a man behind.

Want a weapon! Why, capture one!
Every Doodle has got a gun,
Belt, and bayonet, bright and new;
Kill a Doodle, and capture *two*!

Shoulder to shoulder, son and sire!
All, call all! to the feast of fire!
Mother and maiden, and child and slave,
A common triumph or a single grave.

SOUTHERN SONG
By "L., M.,"

IF ever I consent to be married,
(And who would refuse a good mate?)
The man whom I give my hand to,
Must believe in the rights of the State.

To a husband who quietly submits
To negro-equality sway,
The true Southern girl will not barter
Her heart and affections away.

The heart I may choose to preside o'er
True, warm, and devoted must be,
And have true love for a Union
Under the Southern Liberty Tree.

Should Lincoln attempt to coerce him,
To share with the negro his right,
Then, smiling, I'd gird on his armor,
And bid him God-speed in the fight.

And if he should fall in the conflict,
His memory with tears I will grace;
Better weep o'er a patriot fallen,
Than lush in a Tory embrace.

We girls are all for a Union,
Where a marked distinction is laid
Between the rights of the mistress,
And those of the kinky-haired maid.

THE MARTYR OF ALEXANDRA

Revealed, as in a lightning flash,
A Hero stood!
Th' invading foe, the trumpet's crash,
Set up his blood!

High o'er the sacred pile that bends
  Those forms above,
Thy Star, O Freedom! brightly blends
  Its rays with Love.

The banner of a mighty race
  Serenely there,
Unfurls—the genius of the place,
  And haunted air!

A vow is registered in heaven—
  Patriot! 'twas thine
To guard those matchless colors, given
  By hand Divine.

Jackson! thy spirit may not hear
  The wail ascend!
A nation bends above thy bier,
  And mourns its friend.

Th' example is thy monument;
  In organ tones
Thy name resounds, with glory blent,
  Prouder than thrones!

And they whose loss has been our gain—
  A People's care
Shall win their hearts from pain
  And wipe the tear.

When time shall set the captives free,
  Now scath'd by wrath,—
Heirs of his immortality,
  Bright be their path.

DIXIE
SOUTHRONS. HEAR YOUR COUNTRY CALL YOU!

By Albert Pike

Southrons, hear your Country call you.
   Up! lest worse than death befall you!
      To arms! To arms! To arms! in Dixie!
Lo! all the beacon-fires are lighted,
Let all hearts be now united!

To arms! To arms! To arms! in Dixie.
   Aavance the flag of Dixie!
      Hurrah! hurrah!
For Dixie's land we take our stand,
   And live or die for Dixie!
     To arms! To arms!
        And conquer peace for Dixie!
     To arms! To arms!
        And conquer peace for Dixie!

Hear the Northern thunders mutter!
Northern flags in South wind flutter;
    To arms!
      Advance the flag of Dixie!

Fear no danger! shun no labor!
Lift up rifle, pike, and sabre!
    To arms!
Shoulder pressing close to shoulder.
Let the odds make each heart bolder!
    To arms!
      Advance the flag of Dixie!

How the South's great heart rejoices,
At your cannons' ringing voices;
    To arms!
For faith betrayed and pledges broken,
Wrongs inflicted, insults spoken;
    To arms!
      Advance the flag of Dixie!

Strong as lions, swift as eagles,
Back to their kennels hunt these beagles!
　　To arms!
Cut the unequal words assunder!
Let them then each other plunder!
　　To arms!
　　　　Advance the flag of Dixie!

Swear upon your Country's altar,
Never to submit or alter;
　　To arms!
Till the spoilers are defeated,
Till the Lord's work is completed.
　　To arms!
　　　　Advance the flag of Dixie!

Halt not till our Federation
Secures among Earth's Powers its station!
　　To arms!
Then at peace, and crowned with glory,
Hear your children tell the story;
　　To arms!
　　　　Advance the flag of Dixie!

If the loved ones weep in sadness,
Victory soon shall bring them gladness:
　　To arms!
Exultant pride soon banish sorrow;
Smiles chase tears away to-morow.
　　To arms!
　　　　Advance the flag of Dixie!

TRUE TO HIS NAME

In ancient days, Jehovah said,
　In voice both sweet and calm,
Be Abram's name forever changed
　To that of Abraham!

'Twas then decreed his progeny
    Should occupy high stations,
For Abraham, in Hebrew, means
    "Father of many nations!"

In our own land an Abraham,
    With speeches wise nor witty,
Went down to our Jerusalem,
    The famous Federal city.

True to his name, this Abraham,
    So changed are his relations,
Instead of one great nation, be
    "Father of many nations,"

SOUTHERN WAR-CRY
AIR—"SCOTS, WHA HAE"

Countrymen of Washington!
    Countrymen of Jefferson!
By Old Hick'ry oft led on
    To death or victory!

Sons of men who fought and bled,
Whose blood for you was freely shed,
Where Marion charged and Sumpter led
    For freeman's rights!

From the Cowpens glorious way,
Southern valor led the fray
To Yorktown's eventful day,
    First we were free!

At New Orleans we met the foe;
Oppressors fell at every blow;
There we laid the usurper low,
    For maids and wives!

Who on Palo Alto's day,
'Mid fire and hail at Monterey,
At Buena Vista led the way?
"Rough-and-Ready!"

Southrons all, at Freedom's call,
For our homes united all,
Freemen live, or freemen fall!
Death or liberty!

THE STAR OF THE WEST

I wish I was in de land o' cotton,
   Old times dair ain't not forgotten,—
     Look away,
In Dixie land whar I was born in,
Early on one frosty mornin',—
     Look away,
        Chorus —Den I wish I was in Dixie

In Dixie land dat frosty mornin',
Jis 'bout de time de day was dawnin',
     Look away,
De signal fire from de east bin roarin',
Rouse up, dixie, no more snorin',—
     Look away,
        Den I wish I was in Dixie

Dat rocket high a blazing in de sky,
'Tis de sign dat de snobbies am comin' up nigh.—
     Look away,
Dey bin braggin' long, if we dare too shoot a shot,
Dey comin' up strong and dey'll send us all to pot.
     Fire away, fire away, lads in gray.
        Den I wish I was in Dixie.

TO THE TORIES OF VIRGINIA

In the ages gone by, when Virginia arose
    Her honor and truth to maintain,
Her sons round her banner would rally with pride,
    Determined to save it from stain.

No heart in those days was so false or so cold,
    That it did not exquisitely thrill
With a love and devotion that none would withhold,
    Until death the proud bosom should chill.

Was Virginia in danger? Fast, fast at her call,
    From the mountains e'en unto the sea,
Came up her brave children their mother to shield,
    And to die that she still might be free.

And coward was he, who, when danger's dark cloud
    Overshadowed Virginia's fair sky,
Turned a deaf, careless ear, when her summons was
        heard,
    Or refused for her honor to die.

Oh! proud are the mem'ries of days that are past,
    And richly the heart thrills whene'er
We think of the brave, who, their mother to save,
    Have died, as they lived, without fear.

But *now*, can it be that Virginia's name
    Fails to waken the homage and love
Of e'en one of her sons? Oh! cold, cold must be
    The heart that her name will not move.

When she rallies for freedom, for justice, and right,
    Will her sons, with a withering sneer,
Revile her, and taunt her with treason and shame,
    Or say she is moved by foul fear?

Will they tell her her glories have fled or grown pale?
    That she bends to tyrant in shame?
Will they trample her glorious flag in the dust,
    Or load with reproaches her name?

Will they fly from her shores, or desert her in need?
    Will *Virginians* their backs ever turn

On their mother, and fly when the danger is nigh,
And her claim to their fealty spurn?

False, false is the heart that refuses to yield
The love that Virginia doth claim;
And base is the tongue that could utter the lie,
That charges his mother with shame.

A blot on her 'scutcheon! a stain on her name!
Our heart's blood should wipe it away
We should die for her honor, and count it a boon
Her mandates to heed and obey.

But never, oh, never, let human tongue say
She is false to her honor or fame!
She is true to her past—to her future she's true—
And Virginia has never known shames.

Then shame on the dastard, the recreant fool,
That *would strike, in the dark,* at her now;
That would coldly refuse her fair fame to uphold,
That would basely prove false to his vow.

But no! it cannot—it can never be true,
That Virginia claims one single child,
That would ever prove false to his home or his God,
Or be with foul treason defiled.

And now the man that could succor her enemies now
Even though on her soil he were born,
Is so base, so inhuman, so false, and so vile,
That Virginia disowns him with scorn!

WAR SONG
By A. B. Meek, Of Mobile

Would'st thou have me love thee dearest,
With a woman's proudest heart,
Which shall ever hold thee nearest,
Shrined in its inmost part!

Listen, then! My country's calling
    On her sons to meet the foe!
Leave these groves of rose and myrtle,
    Drop the deamy hand of love!

Like young Korner, scorn the turtle
    When the eagle screams above!
Dost thou pause? Let dotards dally—
    Do thou for thy country fight!

'Neath her noble emblem rally—
    "God! our country, and her fight—
Listen! now her trumpet's calling
    On her sons to meet the foe!

Woman's heart is soft and tender,
    But 'tis proud and faithful, too;
Shall she be her land's defender?
    Lover soldier! up and do!

Seize thy father's ancient falchion,
    Which once flashed as freedom's star!
'Till sweet peace—the bow and halcyon,
    Still'd the stormy strife of war!

Listen! now thy country's calling
    On her sons to meet the foe!
Sweet is love in the moonlight bowers!
    Sweet the altar and the flame!

Sweet is spring-time with her flowers!
    Sweeter far the patriot's name!
Should the God who rules above thee
    Doom thee to a soldier's grave,

Hearts will break, but fame will love thee
    Canonized among the brave!
Listen, then, thy country's calling
    On her sons to meet her foe!

Rather would I view thee lying
    On the last red field of life,
'Mid thy country's heroes dying,
    Than to be a dastard's wife.

FORT SUMTER

It was a noble Roman,
  In Rome's imperial day,
Who heard a coward croaker
  Before the battle say:
"They're safe in such a fortress;
  "There is no way to shake it;"—
"On! on!" exclaimed the hero,
  "I'll find a way, or make it!"

Is fame your aspiration?
  Her path is steep and high;
In vain he seeks the temple,
  Content to gaze and sigh;
The crowded town is waiting,
  But he alone can take it,

Is Glory your ambition?
  There is no royal road;
Alike we all must labor,
  Must climb to her abode;
Who feels the thirst for glory,
  In Helicon may slake it,
If he has but the "Southern will,"
  "To find a way, or make it!"

Is Sumter worth the getting?
  It must be bravely sougth;
With wishing and with fretting
  The boon cannot be bought;
To all the prize is open,
  But only he can take it,
Who says, with "Southern courage,"
  "I'll find a way, or make it!"

In all impassioned warfare,
  The tale has ever been,
That victory crowns the valiant;
  The brave are they who win.
Through strong in "Sumter Fortress,"
  A hero still may take it,
Who says, with "Southern daring,"
  "I'll find a way, or make it!"

REBELS

Rebels! 'tis a holy name!
    The name our fathers bore,
When battling in the cause of Right,
Against the tyrant in his might,
    In the dark days of yore.

Rebels! 'tis our family name!
    Our father, Washington,
Was the arch-rebel in the fight,
And gave the name to us,—a right
    Of father unto son.

Rebels! 'tis our given name!
    Our mother, Liberty,
Received the title with her fame,
    In days of grief, of fear, and shame,
When at her breast were we.

Rebels! 'tis our sealed name!
    A baptism of blood!
The war—aye, and the din of strife—
The fearful contest, life for life—
    The mingled crimson flood.

Rebels! 'tis a patriot's name!
    In struggles it was given;
We bore it then when tyrants raved
And through their curses 't was engraved
    On the doomsday-book of heaven.

Rebels! 'tis our fighting name!
    For peace rules o'er the land,
Until they speak of raven woe—
Until our rights receive a blow,
    From foe's or brother's hand.

Rebels! 'tis our dying name!
    For, although life is dear,
Yet, freemen born and freemen bred
We'd rather live as freemen dead,
    Than live in slavish fear.

Then call us rebels, if you will—
We glory in the name;
For bending under unjust cause,
And swearing faith to unjust laws,
We count a greater shame.

THERE'S NOTHING GOING WRONG
DEDICATED TO "OLD ABE"

There's a general alarm,
The South's begun to arm,
And every hill and glen
Pours forth its warrior men;
Yet, "There's nothing going wrong,"
Is the burden of my song.

Six States already out,
Beckon others on the route;
And the cry is "Still they come!"
From the Southern sunny home;
Yet, "There's nothing going wrong,"
Is the burden of my song.

There's a wail in the land,
From a want-stricken band;
And "Food! Food!" is the cry:
"Give us work or we die!"
Yet, "There's nothing going wrong"
Is the burden of my song.

The sturdy farmer doth complain
Of low prices for his grain;
And the puller, with his flour,
Murmurs the dulness of the hour.
Yet, "There's nothing going wrong,"
Is the burden of my song.

The burly butcher in the mart,
He, too, also takes his port;
And the merchant in his store

Hears no creaking at his door;
But "There nothing going wrong,"
Is the burden of my song.

Stagnation is everywhere;
On the water, in the air,
In the shop, in the forge,
On the mount, in the gorge;
With anvil with the loom,
In the store, and counting-room;
In the city, in the town,
With Mr. Smith, with Mr. Brown!
And "Yet, there's nothing wrong,"
Is the burden of my song.

MARYLAND

By James R. Randall

The despot's heel is on thy shore,
   Maryland!
His torch is at thy temple door,
   Maryland!
Avenge the patriotic gore
That flecked the streets of Baltimore,
And be the battle queen of yore
   Maryland! My Maryland!

Hark to wand'ring son's appeal,
   Maryland!
My mother State! to thee I kneel,
   Maryland!
For life and death, for woe and weal
Thy peerless chivalry reveal,
And gird thy beauteous limbs with steel,
   Maryland! My Maryland!

Thou wilt not cower in the dust,
   Maryland.
Thy beaming sword shall never rest,
   Maryland.

Remember Carroll's sacred crest;
Remember Howard's warlike thrust—
And all thy slumberers with the just,
    Maryland! My Maryland!

Come! 'tis the red dawn of the day,
    Maryland!
Come! with thy panoplied array,
    Maryland.
With Ringgold's spirit for the fray,
With Watson's blood, at Monterey,
With fearless Lowe, and dashing May,
    Maryland! My Maryland.

Come! for thy shield is bright and strong,
    Maryland.
Come! for thy dalliance does thee wrong,
    Maryland.
Come to thine own heroic throng,
That stalks with Liberty along,
And give a new *Key* to thy song,
    Maryland! My Maryland.

Dear Mother! burst the tyrant's chain,
    Maryland.
Virginia should not call in vain,
    Maryland.
She meets her sisters on the plain;
"*Sic semper*," 'tis the proud refrain,
That baffles minions back amain.
    Maryland.
Arise, in majesty again,
    Maryland! My Maryland!

I see the blush upon thy cheek,
    Maryland.
But thou wast ever bravely meek,
    Maryland!
But lo! there surges forth a shriek
From hill to hill, from creek to creek—
Potomac calls to Chesapeake,
    Maryland! My Maryland.

Thou wilt not yield the vandal toil,
Maryland.
Thou wilt not crook to his control,
Maryland.
Better the fires upon thee roll.
Better the blade, the shot, the bowl,
Than crucifixion of the soul,
Maryland! My Maryland.

I hear the distant thunder hum,
Maryland.
The Old Line's bugle, fife and drum,
Maryland.
She is not dead, nor deaf, nor dumb;
Huzza! she spurns the Northern scum!
She breathes—she burns! she'll come! she'll
come:
Maryland! My Maryland.

A CRY TO ARMS

Ho: woodsmen of the mountain side—
Ho—dwellers in the vales;
Ho—ye who by the chafing tide
Have roughened in the gales,
Leave barn and byre, leave kin and cot,
Lay by the spotless spade;
Let desk, and case, and counter rot,
And burn your books of trade.

The despot roves your fairest lands,
And, till he flies or fears,
Your fields must grow but armed hands,
Your sheaves be sheaves of spears.
Give up to mildew and to rust,
The useless tools of gain;
And feed your country's sacred dust,
With floods of crimson rain.

Come, with the weapons at your call—
  With musket, pike, or knife;
He wields the deadliest blade of all
  Who lightest holds his life.
The arm that drives the unbought blows,
  With all a patriots scorn,
Might brain a tyrant with a rose,
  Or stab him with a thorn.

Does any falter? Let him turn
  To some brave maiden's eyes,
And catch the holy fires that bur
  In those sublunar skies.
Oh! could you like your women
  And in their spirit march,
A day might see your lines of steel
  Beneath the victor's arch.

BATTLE ODE TO VIRGINIA

Old Virginia! virgin-crowned
  Daughter of the royal Bess,
Send the fiery ensign round,
Call your chivalry renowned,—
  Lineage of the lioness,

You have thrown the gauntlet down,
  Pledged to vindicate the right;
Bid your sons from field and town,
Through summer's smile and winter's frown,
  Make ready for the fight.

Now that you have drawn the sword,
  Throw away the useless sheath;
Hear your destiny's award,—
Drive the invaders from your sward,
  Or lay your heads beneath.

In the field with conflict rife,
    None must falter, yield, or fly;
Honor, liberty, and life,
All are staked upon the strife;
    You must "do or die."

Let your daughters shed no tear,
    Though their dearest may be slain;
None for self must hope or fear,
All with joy their burdens bear,
    Till you are free again.

By the consecrated soil
    Where your Washington had birth,
Keep your homes from ruthless spoil,
Keep your shield from spot or soil,
    Or perish from the earth.

FLIGHT OF DOODLES

I come from old Manassas, with a pocket full of fun,—
I killed forty yankees with a single-barrelled gun;
It don't make a niff-a-stifference to neither you nor I
Big Yankee, Little Yankee, all run or die.

I saw all the Yankees at Bull Run,
They fought like the devil when the battle first be-
    gun.
But it don't make a niff-a-stifference to neither you
    nor I,
They took to their heels, boys, and you ought to
    see'em fly.

I saw old Fuss-and-Fethers Scott, twenty miles away
His horses stuck up their ears, and you ought to hear
    'em neigh;
But it don't make a niff-a-stifference to neither you
    nor I,
Old Scott fled like the devil, boys; root, hog or die.

I then saw a "Tiger," from the old Crecent City,
He cut down the Yankees without any pity;
Oh! it don't make a diff-a-bitterence to neither you
  nor I,
We whipped the Yankee boys, and made the boobies
  cry.

I saw South Carolina, the first in the cause,
Shake the dirty Yankees till she broke all their jaws;
Oh! don't make a niff-a-stifference to neither you nor I,
South Carolina give 'em——, boys; root hog, or die.

I saw old Virginia, standing firm and true,
She fought mighty hard to whip the dirty crew;
Oh! it don't make a niff-a-stifference to neither you
  nor I,
Old Virginia's blood and thunder, boys; root hog, or
  die.

I saw old Georgia, the next in the van,
She cut down the Yankees almost to a man;
Oh! it don't make a niff-a-stifference to neither you
  nor I,
Georgia's sum in a fight, boys; root, hog, or die.

I saw Alabama in the midst of the storm,
She stood like a giant in the contest so warm;
Oh! it don't make a niff-a-stifference to neither you
  nor I,
Alabama fought the Yankees, boys till the last one
  did fly.

I saw Texas go in with a smile,
But I tell you what it is, she made the Yankees bile;
Oh! it don't make a niff-a-stifference to neither you
  nor I,
Texas is the devil, boys; root, hog, or die.

I saw North Carolina in the deepest of the battle,
She knocked down the Yankees and made their bones
  rattle;
Oh! it don't make a niff-a-stifference to neither you
  nor I,
North Carolina's got the grit, boys; root, hog, or die.

Old Florida came in with a terrible shout,
She frightened all the Yankees till their eyes stuck
    out;
Oh! it don't make a niff-a-difference to neither you
    nor I,
Florida's death on Yankees; root, hog, or die.

CONFEDERATE SONG
AIR—"BRUCE'S ADDRESS"

Rally round our country's flag!
Rally, boy's, nor do not lag;
Come from every vale and crag,
    Sons of Liberty!

Northern Vandals tread our soil,
Forth they come for blood and spoil,
To the homes we've gained with toil,
    Shouting, "Slavery!"

Traitorous Lincoln's bloody band
Now invades the freeman's land,
Arm'd with sword and firebrand,
    'Gainst the brave and free.

Arm ye, then, for fray and fight,
March ye forth both day and night,
Stop not till the foe's in sight,
    Sons of chivalry.

In your veins the blood still flows
Of brave men who once arose—
Burst the shackles of their foes;
    Honest men and free.

Rise, then, in your power and might,
Seek the spoiler, brave the fight;
Strike for God, for Truth for Right:
    Strike for God, for Liberty!

SWEETHEARTS AND THE WAR

Oh, dear! it's shameful, I declare,
    To make the men all go
And leave so many sweethearts here
    Without a single beau.
We like to see them brave, 'tis true,
    And would not urge them stay;
But what are we, poor girls, to do
    When they are all away?

We told them we could spare them there,
    Before they had to go;
But, bless their hearts, we weren't aware
    That we should miss them so.
We miss them all, in many ways
    But truth will ever out,
The greatest thing we miss them for,
    Is seeing us about.

On Sunday, when we go to church,
    We look in vain for some
To meet us, smiling, on the porch,
    And ask to see us home.
And then, we can't enjoy a walk,
    Since all the beaux have gone,
For what's the good, (to use plain talk,)
    If we must trudge alone?

But what's the use of talking thus?
    We'll try to be content;
And if they cannot come to us,
    A message may be sent.
And that's one comfort, any way;
    For though we are apart.
There is no reason why we may
    Not open heart to heart.

We trust it may soon come
    To a final test;
We want to see our Southern homes
    Secured in peaceful rest.

But if the blood of those we love
  In Freedom's cause must flow,
With fervent trust in God above,
  We bid them onward go.

And we will watch them, as they go,
  And cheer them on their way;
Our arms shall be their resting-place
  When wounded sore they lay,
Oh! if the sons of Southern soil
  For Freedom's cause must die,
Her daughters ask no dearer boon
  Than by their side to lie.

"WE COME! WE COME!"
By Millie Mayfield

We come! we come, for Death or Life,
  For the Grave or Victory!
We come to the broad Red Sea of strife,
  Where the black flag waveth free!
We come as Men, to do or die,
  Nor feel that the lot is hard,
When our Hero calls—and our battle-cry
  is "On, to Beauregard!"

Up, craven, up! 'tis no time for ease,
  When the crimson war-tide rolls
To our very doors—up, up, for these
  Are times to try men's soul!
The purple gore calls from the sod
  Of our martyred brothers' grave,
And raises a red right hand to God
  To guard our avenging braves.

And unto the last bright drop that thrills
  The depths of the Southern heart,
We must battle for our sunny hills,
  For the freedom of our Mart—

For all that Honor claims, or Right—
For Country, Love, and Home!
Shout to the trampling steeds of Might
Our cry—"We come! we come!"

And let our path through their serried ranks
Be the fierce tornado's track,
That burst from the torrid's fervid banks
And scatters destruction black!
For the hot life leaping in the veins
Of our young Confedracy
Must break for aye the galling chains
Of dark-brow'd Treachery.

On! on! 'tis our gallant chieftain calls,
(He must not call in vain,)
For aid to guard his homestead walls—
Our Hero of the Plain!
We come! we come, to do or die,
Nor feel that the lot is hard—
"God and our Rights!" be our battle-cry,
And, "On, to Beauregard!"

SONG OF THE SOUTHERN SOLDIER
By P. E. C.

True—"Barclay and Perkins' Drayman"

I'm a soldier, you see, that oppression has made!
I don't fight for pay or booty;
But I wear in my hat a blue cockade,
Placed there by the fingers of Beauty
The South is my home, where a black man is black
And a white man there is a white man;
Now I'm tired of listening to Northern clack,—
Let us see what they'll do in a fight, man!

The Yankees are cute: they have managed somehow
Their business and ours to settle;

They make all we want, from a pin to a plough,
  Now we'll show them some Southern metal.
We have had just enough of their Northern law,
  That robbed us so long of our right, man,
And too much of their cursed abolition jaw,—
  Now we'll see what they'll do in a fight, man,

Their parsons will open their sanctified jaws,
  And cant of our slave-growing sin, sir;
They pocket the profits, while preaching the laws,
  And manage our cotton to spin, sir.
Their incomes ate nice, on our sugar and rice,
  Though against it the hypocrites write, sir;
Now our dander is up, and they'll soon smell a
      mice,
  If we once get them into a fight, sir.

Our cotton bales once made a good barricade,
  Can still do the State a good service;
With them and the boys of the blue cockade,
  There is power enough to preserve us.
So shoulder your rifles, my boys, for defense,
  In the cause of our freedom and right, man;
If there's no other way for to learn them sense,
  We may teach them a lesson in fight, man.

The stars that are growing so fast on our flags,
  We treasure as Liberty's pearls,
And stainless we'll bear them, though shot into
      rags;
  They were fix'd by the hands of our girls.
And fixed stars they shall be in our national sky,
  To guide through the future aright, man,
And young Cousin Sam, with their gleam in his
      eye,
  May dare the whole world to fight, man.

WAR SONG
AIR—"MARCH, MARCH, ETTRICK AND TEVIOTDALE.

March, march on, brave "Palmetto" boys,
"Sumter" and "Lafayettes," forward in order;
March, march, "Calhoun" and "Rifle" boys,
    All the base Yankees are crossing the border.
      Banners are round ye spread,
      Floating above your head,
    Soon shall the Lone Star be famous in story,
      On, on my gallant men,
      Vict'ry be thine again;
    Fight for your rights, till the green sod is gory.
                  March, march.

Young wives and sisters have buckled your armor on;
    Maidens ye love bid ye go to the battle-field;
Strong arms and stout hearts have many a vict'ry
      won,
    Courage shall strengthen the weapons ye wield.
      Wild passions are storming,
      Dark schemes are forming,
    Deep snares are laid, but they shall not enthrall ye;
      Justice your cause shall greet,
      Laurels lay at your feet,
If each brave band be but watchful and wary.
                  March, march.

Let fear and unmanliness vanish before ye;
    Trust in the Rock who will shelter the righteous
Plant firmly each step on the soil of the free,—
    A heritage left by the sires who bled for us.
      May each heart be bounding,
      When trumpets are sounding
    And the dark traitors shall strive to surround ye;
      The great God of Battle
      Can still the war-rattle.
And brighten the laud with a sunset of glory.
                  March, march.

THE DESPOTS SONG
By "Ole Secesh"

With a beard that was filthy and red,
His mouth with tobacco bespread,
Abe Lincoln sat in the gay White House,
A-wishing that he was dead,—
Swear! swear! swear!
Till his tongue was blistered o'er;
Then, in a voice not very strong,
He slowly whimed the Despot's song—

Lie! lie! lie!
I've lied like the very deuce
Lie! lie! lie!
As long as lies were of use;
But now that lies no longer pay,
I know not where to turn;
For when I her truth would say,
My tongue with lies will burn!

Drink! drink! drink!
Till my head feels very queer!
Drink! drink! drink!
Till I get rid of all fear!
Brandy, and whiskey, and gin,
Sherry, and champagne, and pop,
I tipple, I guzzle, I suck 'em all in,
Till down dead-drunk I drop.

Think! think! think!
Till my head is very sore!
Think! think! think!
Till I couldn't think any more!
And it's oh! to be splitting of rails,
Back in my Illinois hut;
For now that everything fails,
I would of my office be "shut!"

Jeff! Jeff! Jeff!
To you as a suppliant I kneel!
Jeff! Jeff! Jeff!
If you could my horrors feel,

You'd submit at discretion,
And kindly give in
To all my oppression,
My weakness and sin!

THE SOUTHERN'S WAR-SONG
By J. A. Wagner

Arise! arise! with main and might,
Sons of the sunny clime!
Gird on the sword; the sacred fight
The holy hour doth chime.
Arise! the craven host draws nigh,
In thundering array;
Arise, ye brave! let cowards fly—
The hero bides the fray.

Strike hard, strike hard, thou noble band;
Strike hard, with arm of fire!
Strike hard, for God and fatherland,
For mother, wife, and sire!
Let the thunders roar, the lightning flash;
Bold Southern, never fear!
The bay'net's point, the sabre's clash,
True Southrons do and dare!

Bright flowr's spring from the hero's grave;
The craven knows no rest!
Thrice curs'd the traitor and the knave!
The hero thrice is bless'd.
Then let each noble Southern stand,
With bold and manly eye;
We'll do for God and Fatherland!
We'll do, we'll do or die!

JUSTICE IS OUR PANOPLY
By DE G.

We're free from Yankee despots,
  We've left the foul mud-sills,
Declared for e'er our freedom,—
  We'll keep it spite of ills.

Bring forth your scum and rowdies,
  Thieves, vagabonds, and all;
March down your Seventh Regiment,
  Battalions great and small.

We'll meet you in Virginia,
  A Southern battle-field,
Where Southern men will never
  To Yankees foemen yield.

Equip your Lincoln cavalry,
  Your negro light-brigade,
Your hodmen, bootblacks, tinkers,
  And scum of every grade.

Pretended love for negroes
  Invites you to the strife;
Well, come each Yankee white man,
  And take a negro wife.

You'd make fit black companions,
  Black heart joined to black skin
Such unions would be glorious—
  They'd make the Devil grin.

Our freedom is our panoply—
  Come on, you base black-guards,
We'll snuff you like wax-candles,
  Led by our Beauregards.

P. G. T. B. is not alone,
  Men like him with him fight;
God's providence is o'er us,
  He will protect the right.

LINCOLN'S INAUGURAL ADDRESS
"IN ADVANCE OF ALL COMPETITORS"

BY A "SOUTHERN RIGHS" MAN

Come at the peoples's mad-jority call,
To open the Nation's quarternary ball,
And invite black and white to fall into ranks,
To dance a State jig on Republican planks.

I'll fiddle like Nero, when Rome was on fire,
And play any tune that the people desire.
So let us be merry,—whatever the clatter be,—
Whilst playing; "O dear! O me! what can the
    matter be?"

I've made a great speech for the people's diversion,
And talked about billet-doux, love, and coercion;
Of the spot I was born, of the place I was reared,
And the girl that I kissed on account of my beard.

I'll settle the tariff—there's no one can doubt it,
But, as yet, I know nothing or little about it;
And as for those Southerns' bluster and clatter,
I know very well that there's nothing the matter.

You've oft heard repeated those wonderful tales
Of my beating a giant in splitting up rails;
And ere I left home—you know the fact is true—
That I beat a small Giant at politics, too.

Should it now be the will of the North and the
    Fates,
I can do it up Brown, by the splitting of States;
And then, when the State-splitting business fails
I'll resume my old trade as a splitter of rails.

THE CALL OF FREEDOM

Har'r! to the rescue! Freedom calls,
  Where triumph's banners brightly wave,
And triumphs he who nobly falls,
  For glory gilds his honored grave!
But fall he will not, if on high
  Still rules the mighty and the Just,
Or, daring thus, if doom'd to die,
  The tyrant first shall bite the dust!

Virginia Queen of nations proud!
  How grand in all the classic past!
Thine offspring, Freedom, calls aloud,
  And Honor echoes back the blast!
The fame of all thine ancient years,
  The demigods of olden time,
Dispel the dastard dream of fears,
  And dare thee act thy part sublime.

Virginia answers to the call!
  Virginia, ever great and free:
The brave, the beautiful, and all
  From mountain crag, and teeming vale,
From every humble hamlet home,
  As swift as sweeps the lightning gale,
Her stalwart children, crowding, come!

They come! they come! devoutly fired,
  To do or die, in Freedom's cause;
By justice armed, by God inspired,
  To vindicate their sovereign laws!
And Heaven will shield the honored breast
  That braves the tyrant's stripes unfurl'd
And victory o'er that banner rest,
  Whose dawning splendors fill the world!

All proudly gleams the golden dawn,
  The starred Aurora of the free;
All brightly bursts the blazing morn
  Of fixed and faithful Liberty.
For ever flame that standard high
  O'er mountain crest and surging stream,
Where courage, faith, and purity,
  In loving lustres blending beam!

In Southern skies, on Southern soil,
O'er honest Southern heads and hearts,
For all who think, for all who toil,
Till life's last lingering drop departs,
Shall grandly wave in glory bright,
From gulf to bay, from sea to sea,
In one undying blaze of light,
That noblest ensign of the free.

By all that woman's love inspires,
By all that breathes above the sod,
By the fond ashes of our sires,
By the eternal truth of God,
Where land the felons but to die,
Their footsteps first shall be their last!
Their base-born blood shall shock the sky!
And havoc shudder back agast!

Hark! to the rescue. Freedom calls,
Where Freedom's banners brightly wave,
And triumphs he who nobly falls,
For glory gild his honored grave!
But fall he will not, if on high
Still rules the mighty and the Just,
Or, daring thus, if doom'd to die,
The tyrant first shall bite the dust!

MANASSAS
By A Rebel

Upon our country's border lay,
Holding the ruthless foe at bay,
Through chilly night and burning day,
Our army at Manassas.

Then our eager eyes were turned,
While many restless spirits burned,
And many a fond heart wildly yearned,
O'er loved ones at Manassas.

For fast the Vandals gathered, strong
In wealth and numbers, all along
Our highways pressed a countless throng,
    To battle at Manassas.

With martial pomp and proud array,
With burnished arms and banners gay,
Panting for the inhuman fray,
    They rolled upon Manassas.

The opening cannons' thunders rent
The air, and ere their charge was spent,
Muskets and rifles quickly sent
    Death to us at Manassas.

But, like a wall of granite, stood
The true, the great, the brave, the good,
Who firmly holding field and wood,
    Guarded us at Manassas.

They promptly answered fire with fire;
Danger could not with fear inspire
Their hearts, whose courage rose the higher,
    When death ruled at Manassas.

At dawn the murderous work begun;
The battle fiercely raged at noon;
Evening drew on,—'t was not done,—
    The carnage at Manassas.

Oh, trembling Freedom! didst thou stay
Throughout that agonizing day,
To watch where victory would lay
    Her laurels at Manassas!

Yes! and thy potent trumpet tone
Ordered our gallant warriors on,
To the bold charge which for thee won
    The triumph at Manassas.

Well might the dastard foemen yield,
When Right and Vengeance joined to wield
The well-aimed ball and glittering steel,
    Which followed up their wild retreat,—

They broke, and fear lent wings to feet,
Flying before our charges fleet,
Which followed up their wild retreat,—
    Their mad rout at Manassas.

Strike! Southrons, strike! for ne'er a foe
So worthy of your every blow
Can your good swords and carbines know,
    As those who south Manassas.

For that our homes are still secure,
Our wives and sisters still left pure,
Our altars drip not with our gore;
    Thanks, victors of Manassas!

Thy charmed trumpet sound, O Fame
Let music catch the loud refrain,
While in a glad, triumphant strain,
    We celebrate Manassas.

And every soldier's breast shall fire
With emulation, and desire
To equal—fame can point no higher—
    The heroes of Manassas.

Alas! that many writhe in pain,
Whose precious blood was spilt to gain
Glory and freedom on thy plain,—
    Thy bloody plain, Manassas.

If sympathy can aught avail,
If fervent prayers with Heaven prevail,
In your behalf they shall not fail,
    Poor wounded of Manassas.

Alas! that blended with the tone
Of triumph, breathes the stifled moan
For many brave, whose dear lives won
    The victory of Manassas.

A grateful nation long shall keep
Their memory, and flock to weep
Above the turf where softly sleep
    The martyrs of Manassas.

SOUTHERN SONG
TUNE—"WAIT FOR THE WAGON"

Come, all ye sons of freedom,
And join our Southern band,
We are going to fight the Yankees,
And drive them from our land.
Justice is our motto,
And Providence our guide,
So jump into the wagon,
And we'll all take a ride,
Chorus—So wait for the wagon! the
dissolution wagon;
The South is the wagon, and we'll all
take a ride.

Secession is our watchword;
Our rights we all demand;
To defend our homes and firesides
We pledge our hearts and hands,
Jeff. Davis is our President,
With Stephens by his side;
Great Beauregard our General;
He joins us in our ride.
Chorus—Wait for the wagon, &tc.

Our wagon is the very best;
The running gear is good;
Stuffed round the sides with cotton,
And made of Southern wood.
Carolina is the driver,
With Georgia by her side;
Virginia hold the flag up
While we all take a ride.
Chorus—Wait for the wagon, &tc.

The invading tribe, called Yankees,
With Lincoln for their guide
Tried to keep Kentucky
From joining in the ride;
But she heeded not their entreaties,—
She has come into the ring;
She wouldn't fight for a government
Where cotton wasn't king.
Chorus—So wait for the wagon, &tc.

Old Lincoln and his Congressmen
  With Seward by his side,
Put old Scott in the wagon,
  Just for to take a ride.
McDowell was the driver,
  To cross Bull Run he tried,
But there he left the wagon
  For Beauregard to ride.
      Chorus—Wait for the wagon, &tc.

Manassas was the battle ground;
  The field was fair and wide:
The Yankees thought they'd whip us out,
  And on to Richmond ride;
But when they met our "Dixie" boys,
  Their danger they espied;
They wheeled about for Washington,
  And didn't wait to ride.
      Chorus—So wait for the wagon, &tc.

Brave Beauregard, God bless him!
  Let legions in his stead,
While Johnson seized the colors
  And waved them o'er his head.
To rising generations,
  With pleasure we will tell
How bravely our Fisher
  And gallant Johnson fell.
      Chorus—So wait for the wagon, &tc.

YANKEE VANDALS

AIR—"GAY AND HAPPY"

The Northern Abolition vandals,
Who have come to free the slave,
Will meet their doom in "Old Virginny,"
Where they all well get a grave.
  Chorus. So let the yankees say what they will,
    We'll love and fight for Dixie still,
    Love and fight for love and fight for,
    We'll love and fight for Dixie still.

They started for Manassas Junction,
With an army full of fight,
But they caught a Southern tartar,
And they took a bully fight.
    So let the Yankees, etc.

"Old Fuss and Feathers" could not save them,
All their boasting was in vain,
Before the Southern steel they cowered,
And their bodies strewed the plain.
    So let the Yankees, etc.

The "Maryland Line" was there as ever,
With their battle-shout and blade,
They shed new lustre on their mother,
When that final charge they made.
    So let Yankees, etc.

Old Abe may make another effort
For to take his onward way,
But his legions then as ever,
Will be forced to run away.
    So let the Yankees, etc.

Brave Jeff. and glorious Beauregard,
With dashing Johnson, noble, true,
Will meet their hireling host again,
And scatter them like morning dew.
    So let the Yankees, etc.

When the Hessian horde is driven,
O'er Potomac's classic flood,
The pulses of a new-born freedom,
Then will stir old Maryland's blood.
    So let the Yankees, etc.

From the lofty Alleghanies,
To old Worchester's sea-washed shore,
Her sons will come to greet the victors,
There in good old Baltimore.
    So let the Yankees, etc.

When with voices light and gladsome,
We will swell the choral strain,
Telling that our dear old mother,
Glorious Maryland's free again.
    So let the yankees, etc.

Then we'll crown our warrior chieftains,
Who have led us in the fight,
And have brought the South in Triumph
Through dread danger's troubled night.
    So let the Yankees, etc.

And the brave who nobly perished,
Struggling in the bloody fray,
We'll weave a wreath of fadeless laurel
For their glorious memory.
    So let the Yankees, etc.

O'er their graves the Southern maidens,
From sea-shore to mountain grot,
Will plant the smiling rose of beauty,
And the sweet forget-me-not.
    So let the Yankees, etc.

THE SOLDIER BOY
By H. M. L.

I give my soldier boy a blade,
    In fair Damascus fashioned well;
Who first the glittering falchion swayed,
    Who first beneath its fury fell.
I know not; but I hope to know
    That for no mean of hireling trade,
To guard no feeling, base or low,
    I give my soldier boy a blade.

Cool, calm, and clear, the lucid flood;
    In which its tempering work was done!
As calm, as clear, as clear of mood
    Be thou when'er it sees the sun;

For country's claim, at honor's call,
  For outraged friend, insulted maid,
At mercy's voice to bid it fall,
  I give my soldier boy a blade.

The eye which marked its peerless edge,
  The hand that weigh'd its balanced poise
Anvil and pincers, forgo and wedge,
  Are gone with all their flame and noise;
And still the gleaming sword remaińs.
  So when in dust I low am laid,
Remember by these heartfelt strains,
  I give my soldier boy a blade.

A SOUTHERN GATHERING SONG
By L. Virginia French

Air—"Hail Columbia"

Song of the South, beware the foe!
Hark to the murmur deep and low,
Rolling up like the coming storm,
Swelling up like the sounding storm,
Hoarse as the hurricanes that brood
In space's far infinitude!
Minute guns of omen boom
Through the future's folded gloom;
Sounds prophetic fill the air,
Heed the warning—and prepare!
  Watch! be wary—every hour
  Mark the foeman's gathering power—
  Keep watch and ward upon his track
  And crush the rash invader back!

Sons of the Brave!—a barrier stanch
Breasting the ailen avalanche—
Manning the battlements of right;
Up, for our Country, "God, and right!"
From your battalions steadly,

And strike for death or victory!
Surging onward sweeps the wave,
Serried columns of the brave,
Banded 'neath the bension
Of Freedom's godlike Washington!
  Stand! but should the invading foe
  Aspire to lay your altars low,
  Charge on the tyrant ere he gain
  Your iron arteried domain!

Sons of the brave! when tumult trod
The tide of revolution—God
Looked from His throne on "the things of time,"
And two new stars in the rein of time
He bade to burn in the azure dome—
The freeman's love and the freeman's home!
Holy of holies! guard them well,
Baffle the despot's secret spell,
And let the chords of life be riven
Eae you yield those gifts of Heaven
  Io *poean*! trumpet notes
  Shake the air where our banner floats;
  Io triumphe! still we see
  The land of the South is the home of the free!

ANOTHER YANKEE DOODLE

Yankee Doodle had a mind
  To whip the Southern traitors,
Because they didn't choose to live
  On codfish and potatoes.
Yankee Doodle, doodle-doo,
  Yankee Doodle dandy,
And so to keep his courage up
  He took a drink of brandy.

Yankee Doodle said he found
  By all the census figures,
That he could starve the rebels out,
  If he could steal their niggers.

Yankee Doodle, doodle-doo,
Yankee Doodle dandy,
And then he took another drink
Of gunpowder and brandy.

Yankee Doodle made a speech;
'Twas very full of feeling;
I fear, says he, I cannot fight,
But I am good at stealing.
Yankee Doodle, doodle-doo,
Yankee Doodle dandy,
Hurrah for Lincoln, he's the boy
To take a drop of brandy.

Yankee Doodle drew his sword,
And practised all the passes;
Come, boys, we'll take another drink
When we get to Manassas.
Yankee Doodle, doodle-doo,
Yankee Doodle dandy,
They never reached Manassas plain,
And never got the brandy.

Yankee Doodle soon found out
That Bull Run was no trifle;
For if the North knew how to steal,
The South knew how to rifle.
Yankee Doodle, doodle-doo,
Yankee Doodle dandy,
'Tis very clear I took too much
Of that infernal brandy.

Yankee Doodle wheeled about,
And scampered off at full run,
And such a race was never seen
As that he made at Bull Run.
Yankee Doodle, doodle-doo,
Yankee Doodle dandy,
I havn't time to stop just now
To take a drop of brandy.

Yankee Doodle, oh! for shame,
Your're always intermeddling;
Let guns alone, they're dangerous things;
You'd better stick to peddling,

Yankee Doodle, doodle-doo,
Yankee Doodle dandy,
When next I go to Bully Run
I'll throw away the brandy.

Yankee Doodle, you had ought
To be a little smarter;
Instead of catching woolly heads,
I vow you've caught a tartar.
Yankee Doodle, doodle-doo,
Yankee Doodle dandy,
Go to hum, youv'e had enough
Of rebels and of brandy.

THE STARS AND BARS

'Tis sixty-two!—and sixty-one,
With the old Union now is gone,
Reeking with bloody wars—
Gone with that ensign, once so prized,
The Stars and Stripes, now so despised,
Struck for the Stars and Bars.

The burden once of patriot's song,
Now badge of tyranny and wrong,
For us no more it waves;
We claim the stars—the stripes we yield,
We give *them* up on every field,
Where fight the Southern braves.

Our motto thus—"God and our Right;"
For sacred liberty we fight—
Not for the lust of power;
Compelled by wrongs the sword t' unsheath,
We'll fight, be free, or cease to breathe—
We'll die before we cower.

By all the blood our fathers shed,
We will from tyranny be freed—
We will not conquered be;

Like them, no higher power we own
But God's—we how to Him alone—
   We will, we will be free!

For homes and altars we contend,
Assured that God will us defend—
   He makes our cause His own;
Not of our gallant patriot host,
Not of brave leader do we boast
   We trust in God alone.

Sumter, and Bethel, and Bull Run
Witnessed fierce battles fought and won,
   By aid of Power Divine;
We met the foe, who us defied,
In all his pomp, in all his pride,
   Shouting: "Manasseh's mine!"

It was not thine, thou boasting foe!
We laid thy vandal legions low,
   We made them bite the sod;
At Lexington the braggart yields,
Leesburg, Belmont, and other fields;—
   Still help us, mighty God!

Thou smiled'st on the patriot seven,
Thou smiled'st on the brave eleven
   Free, independent States;
Their number Thou wilt soon increase,
And bless them with a lasting peace,
   Within their happy gates.

No more shall violence then be heard,
Wasting destruction no more feared
   In all this Southern land;
"Praise," she her gates devoutly calls,
"Salvation," her heaven-guarded walls,
   What shall her power withstand?

"The little one," by heavenly aid,
"A thousand is—the small one made,
   "A nation—oh! how strong!"
Jehovah, who the right befriends,
Jehovah, who our flag defends,
   Is hastening it along!

OUR BRAVES IN VIRGINIA

Air—"Dixie Land"

We have ridden from the brave Southwest,
On fiery steeds, with throbbing breast;
    Hurrah! hurrah! hurrah! hurrah!
With sabre flash and rifle true,
    Hurrah! hurrah!
The Northern ranks we will cut through,
  And charge for old Virginia, boys.
    Hurrah! hurrah!
  Then charge for Old Virginia.

We have come from the cloud-capp'd mountains,
From the land of purest fountains;
    Hurrah! hurrah! hurrah! hurrah!
Our sweethearts and wives conjure us,
    Hurrah! hurrah!
Not to leave a foe before us,
  And strike for old Virginia, boys, &c.

Then we'll rally to the bugle call,
For Southern rights we'll fight and fall;
    Hurrah! hurrah! hurrah! hurrah!
Our gray-haired sires sternly say,
    Hurrah! hurrah!
That we must die or win the day.
  Three cheers for Old Virginia, &c.

Then our silken banner wave on high;
For Southern homes we'l fight and die.
    Hurrah! hurrah! hurrah! hurrah!
Our cause is right, our quarrel just,
    Hurrah! hurrah!
We'll in the God of battles trust,
  And conquer for Virginia, boys, &c.

THE SONG OF THE EXILE
AIR: "DIXIE"

Oh! here I am in the land of cotton,
The flag once honored is now forgotten;
    Fight away, fight away, fight away for Dixie's land.
But here I stand for Dixie dear,
To fight for freedom, without fear;
    Fight away, fight away, fight away for Dixie's land.
    Chorus. For Dixie's land I'll take my stand,
        To live or die for Dixie's land.
        Fight away, fight away, fight away for
        Dixie's land.

Oh! have you heard the latest news,
Of Lincoln and his kangaroos;
    Fight away, &c.
His minions now they would oppress us,
With war and bloodshed they'd distress us!
    Fight away, &c.

Abe Lincoln tore through Baltimore,
In a baggage-car with fastened door;
    Fight away, etc.
And left his wife alas! alack!
To perish on the railroad track!
    Fight away, etc.

Abe Lincoln is the President,
He'll wish his days in Springfield spent;
    Fight away, etc.
We'll show him that old Scott's a fool,
We'll ne'er submit to Yankee rule,
    Fight away, etc.

At first our States were only seven,
But now we number stars eleven
    Fight away, etc.
Brave old Missouri shall be ours,
Despite old Lincoln's Northern powers,
    Fight away, etc.

We have no ships, we have no navies,
But mighty faith in the great Jeff. Davis,
    Fight away, etc.

Due honor, too, we will award,
To gallant Bragg and Beauregard,
    Fight away, etc.

Abe's proclamation in a twinkle,
Stirred up the blood of Rip Van Winkle;
    Fight away, etc.
Jeff. Davis's answer was short and curt:
"Fort Sumter's taken and 'nobody's hurt!"
    Fight away, etc.